TO REACH THE CLOUDS

Books
Trois Coups
On the High Wire
Traité du Funambulisme
Funambule

Major Performances
Cathedral of Notre-Dame
Sydney Harbour Bridge
World Trade Center
Cathedral Church of St. John the Divine
Paris Opera
Museum of the City of New York
Lincoln Center
Jerusalem (A Bridge for Peace)
Grand Central Terminal
Eiffel Tower
Tokyo, Akasaka
Vienna Film Festival
Frankfurt Cathedral
American Museum of Natural History
Crossing Broadway, New York City

Works in Progress
Canyon Walk
The Sydney Walk
Easter Island Walk

Films with Philippe Petit
Concert in the Sky
High Wire
Niagara: Miracles, Myths & Magic
Tour et Fil
Werner Herzog's Filmstunde
National Geographic Profile of Philippe Petit
The Man on the Wire
Historischer Hochseillauf
Mondo
Nova's Secrets of the Lost Empire

TO REACH THE CLOUDS

MY HIGH-WIRE WALK
BETWEEN THE TWIN TOWERS

PHILIPPE PETIT

faber and faber

First published in Great Britain in 2003
by Faber and Faber Limited
3 Queen Square, London WC1N 3AU
Published in the United States in 2002 by North Point Press
A division of Farrar, Straus and Giroux, New York

Typeset by Faber and Faber Limited
Printed in England by Clays Ltd, St Ives plc

All rights reserved

© Philippe Petit, 2002

The right of Philippe Petit to be identified as author of this work
has been asserted in accordance with Section 77 of the
Copyright, Designs and Patent Act 1988

ILLUSTRATION CREDITS
© 2002 by Jean-Louis Blondeau / POLARIS IMAGES:
pp. 86, 162, 164–63, 169, 173, 174, 176–77, 180, 183, 186–87

© 2002 by Jim Moore / POLARIS IMAGES:
pp. xii–xiii, 16, 18, 28, 32, 35, 63, 69, 213

© 1982 Fred Conrad / *The New York Times*, p. 212

© 1974 Vic DeLuca / *New York Post* REX USA, p. 189

Collection of the author: all documents, and photographs
on pp. 2, 5, 23, 37, 47, 71, 92, 102, 109, 111, 121, 195, 197, 209;
by Annie Allix, p. 102; by Jean-Pierre Dousseau, pp. 170, 171;
by Judy Finelly, pp. 11, 90; by Jean-Michel Folon, p. 215;
by Loretta Harris, p. 84; by Jean-François Heckel, p. 167;
by Jacques Pavlowsky, p. 9 (top); by James Ricketson, p. 9 (bottom);
stills from 16mm film by Yves Bourde, pp. 53, 57.
All sketches and drawings are by the author.

A CIP record for this book
is available from the British Library

ISBN 0–571–21770–2

2 4 6 8 10 9 7 5 3 1

One more thing: Philippe, you are not a coward – so what I
want to hear from you is the ecstatic truth about the twin towers.

WERNER HERZOG

This story is dedicated to Jean-Louis Blondeau

and belongs to Jim Moore,

Annie Allix,
Jean-François Heckel,

Papa Rudy,
Francis Brunn,
Barry Greenhouse,
Jean-Pierre Dousseau,

Ann Forster,
Jessica Lange,
Rick Schneider,
Mark Lewis,
Paul Frame,
Judy Bohannon and my friend Baron,
Loretta Harris,
Pat Pannel,
Alain Ballini,
Oscar Figueroa,
Philippe Rodier,
Yves Bourde,

and to that seabird circling over me on the morning of
August 7, 1974.

As for the false friends who helped and gave up, who helped
and betrayed, they are merely guilty of not having had enough
heart to move mountains. I forgive you. This is why I changed
your names in the text and blackened your eyes
in the photographs—to confuse the gods.
Perhaps they will not recognize you.

This book is dedicated to
my ever-generous partner in crime,
thought-provoking longtime companion,
trusted in-house editor, and gifted cook,
Kathy O'Donnell

CONTENTS

X

TO REACH THE CLOUDS

Rebel poet?

By four years old, disdain for my fellow man starts to show: I climb onto everything to distance myself. At age six, I announce, "When I grow up, I want to be a theatrical director!" Then I proceed to learn magic on my own.

During the next ten years, I study drawing, painting, sculpting, fencing, printing, carpentry, theater, and horseback riding, all with prestigious masters; I embrace focus, tenacity, respect for the tool, and passion.

The reaction of my parents to my unruly individuality is to legally emancipate me on my seventeenth birthday. Autodidact, I become a juggler and a tightrope walker.

By the time I turn eighteen, I've been expelled from five schools for practicing the art of the pickpocket on my teachers and the art of card manipulation under my desk. I refuse to take the basic exam to prove I can read, write, and count, and thereby jeopardize my chances of landing a job picking up garbage or operating a cash register. Instead, I leave home and become a wandering troubadour, a street-juggler without a permit who is arrested constantly . . . all over the world.

No one wishes to hire me, practitioner of an absurd arrogance; for a while I make sure it stays that way. It becomes essential to write, play chess, learn Russian and bullfighting, discover architecture and engineering, invent hiding places, erect tree houses, train at lock-picking—to indulge my gourmandise for knowledge while honing my perfectionism.

This course of events conduces me to imagine rigging a wire in secret somewhere and performing on such an imposed stage, out of reach, in total disregard of the powers that be.

The adventure of the World Trade Center begins with the first appearance of such thoughts, in a dentist's waiting room in Paris. I am barely eighteen years old.

TOOTHACHE

I am barely eighteen years old, free, rebellious, and untrusting. It's winter in Paris, 1968.

Pain from multiple cavities forces me to enter a dentist's waiting room. The air is stale, the ceiling low, the wallpaper hideous. A couple of naked forty-watt bulbs reveal half a dozen senior citizens, who greet my entrance with loathing and suspicion.

I grab a stack of outdated newspapers and flip the pages as noisily as possible. Suddenly, there is silence: I am staring at an illustration and reading over and over a short article about a fantastic building whose twin towers, 110 stories tall, will rise over New York City in a few years and "tickle the clouds."

Over the photograph of the architect's model, in a display of classic French chauvinism, an outline of the Eiffel Tower has been superimposed at the same scale, for comparison. On the side, the pitiful Tour Maine Montparnasse, unknown to the world yet Parisians' latest pride, stands less than half the size of the American project. With typical French egocentricity, a large heading proclaims, 100 METERS MORE THAN THE EIFFEL TOWER, while a subheading informs us erroneously, IT'S THE "TRADE WORLD CENTER" OF NEW YORK.

Although I have been practicing only a few months, I have already announced my intention to become high wire artist supreme, and wire walking has already become my obsessive, nearly fanatical new passion. So it is as a reflex that I take the pencil from behind

4

100 mètres de plus que la tour Eiffel

C'EST LE "TRADE WORLD CENTER" DE NEW YORK

my ear to trace a line between the two rooftops—a wire, but no wirewalker.

I want this article. I need this article.

It is almost a crime in my country to deprive a professional antechamber of useless reading material, and almost certainly another to tear out a page.

I begin to stare with growing intensity at the cheap reproduction of *Les Nymphéas* hanging askew above the grandfather clock, as if a huge insect were strolling across the canvas. Soon, necks twisted, everyone joins me in staring at the painting. I let go of a giant "Aa-choo!" that gives me cover as I tear the page and shove it under my jacket, then hurriedly disappear.

The heist takes less than a second. It takes me a week to find another dentist, but the pain I suffer is nothing compared to the dream freshly acquired.

If this were a scene from my film, I would have the camera follow the clipping back to the young thief's studio, show the document being pulled out from under his jacket—tight frame—and being filed inside a large red box dragged from under his bed. A close-up would reveal the box's label in boldface Garamond: PROJECTS.

These files are not business ventures, but projects that ripen in the clouds. The secret desires of children who spend afternoons in treetops. Dreams.

And yet I will forget the clipping, for much of the next four years . . .

TO REACH THE CLOUDS

During the next few years, unbeknownst to me and thousands of miles away, something amazing, something unheard of, something colossal is happening.

First an architect had a vision. A preliminary model, eight feet high, was constructed; another dozen, at different scales, would follow. Little sketches gave way to drawings of great detail and dimension, thousands of them. In downtown Manhattan, thirteen city blocks would have to be cleared. Ground was broken.

Now imagine!

Hundreds of men, trusting only those childish cardboard-and-glue assemblies, guided only by those pitiful sheets of flammable paper marked with thin blue lines, hundreds of men are leading thousands of men, men with tools, men with machines, into stacking steel, concrete, aluminum, and glass in perfect balance and in total disregard of the commandment, "Thou shall not try to reach the clouds."

The ants are building a skyscraper—a skyscraper with two arms, pointing at the gods.

The rest is noise, lots of noise. The cranes are slewing, luffing, and lifting 192,000 tons of steel. Each I-beam, each load-bearing column tree, each truss is numbered by hand before being slung and sent into the sky. And someone always knows precisely how and when to connect the pieces.

This goes on for three years.

And the twin towers rise.

NOTRE-DAME AND SYDNEY HARBOUR BRIDGE

Because I live on rue Laplace, the towers of the nearby cathedral watch me come and go every day. One afternoon they call to me.

I take a few measurements in secret, inspect areas not open to tourists, plan a nocturnal rigging, convince a few friends to become accomplices.

Paris is asleep.

My false key allows us to reach the top of the towers. One of my juggling balls, tied to a fishing line, is thrown across. We install the steel cable all night.

Paris is awake.

I promenade and daydream 250 feet in the air on this twenty-sixth of June, 1971—my first illegal aerial performance.

The romantic escapade ends up on front pages everywhere; the world salutes the valiant young poet. Except the French, who are not touched, not enthused. They do not need an encore.

Disgusted, I depart for Australia. In Sydney, I improvise another surprise, a walk between the northern pylons of the world's largest steel arch bridge, on the third of June, 1973.

Without these first clandestine walks, would I have reached inside the red box for a more formidable opponent?

PARIS MATCH, 1972

Sometime between Notre-Dame and Sydney Harbour Bridge, an alarming article appears, tucked away in the back of a magazine. It tells of two pillars already towering above lower Manhattan. A full-page aerial shot portrays the towers as if they were already out of reach. I can hear the cranes bustling to complete the structure on schedule. I can smell the smoke, feel the incessant activity, the urgency . . .

The article is so disturbing that I throw it into the large red box labeled PROJECTS and try to forget about it.

I cannot.

The towers keep erupting in my conversations, my thoughts, my dreams.

How were they born without warning?

Why didn't I hear the town crier shouting the news on rue Laplace: "The towers are being built! The towers are being built!"

What if they are completed before I link them for eternity? I must keep an eye on them. Once they are officially opened, it may be impossible to take them by surprise.

Alarming, indeed.

"I'M GOING TO AMERICA!"

I'm tired of the French. The zeal of the Parisian police and the constant wet and cold have curtailed my street performances so drastically that I decide to try New York City. Am I being influenced by my new, first-time-in-Paris American girlfriends, adorable Jessica and her suave companion, Ann? After each of my juggling circles, they tell me, "No one does that in New York, they'll love you over there!" Or is it the offer Ann whispers as she heads back to the States, to share her East 96th Street apartment?

January 6, 1974, I pack my bags and go up to the roof to scream, "I'm going to America!"

I have locked up my room at rue Laplace and am almost downstairs when I suddenly run back up. From under the bed I pull out the red box and retrieve the skyscraper clippings. You never know . . .

Two hours later, I board the plane with my top hat on and my antique postal bag over my shoulder, pushing my unicycle.

It's even colder in New York.

Who cares? I'm delighted to be able to juggle under a new sky, in front of new people.

The first circle of chalk I draw on Manhattan asphalt is between Patience and Fortitude, the stone lions trying to pass for sphinxes on the front steps of the public library. And the first spectator to throw a buck into my hat is . . . Francis Brunn, the

greatest juggler of all time, my friend! "But I thought you were in Barcelona!" We hug, we laugh. We meet only by accident, by miracle.

Several other people in the crowd approach me. I remember the warm handshake of a muscular young man standing very straight, like a dancer: Jim Moore, mime-photographer. We promise to meet again.

I persuade Francis to stroll with me in the snow. We have so many stories to trade. I let him know I already adore this frightening metropolis, and I confess, "One day New York will be mine! I'll string a wire somewhere between the tallest buildings and I will become the king of the American sky!" He believes me, I know; his laughter proves it.

The next evening after street-juggling, I return to 59 East 96th Street to find a huge cockroach in the kitchen—never heard of them in Paris, never met one before! I record in my datebook my first impression of New York: "It's old, it's dirty, it's full of sky-scrapers. I love it."

With performances, my new friends, and my appetite to devour Manhattan, I keep forgetting the towers' existence. Nearly three weeks later, just days before I am to return to France, I force myself to go meet them. Since I'm far up the immense oblong island, and they happen to live near the bottom, the price of the encounter is a forty-five-minute subterranean journey.

FIRST VISION, FIRST VISIT

Without warning, at five o'clock on the afternoon of the corrida, the bull is let out of the dark cell where he has been confined without food for days. Enraged, he springs onto unknown sand, eager to fight, only to find scorching sun above, and screaming voices. He is blind. He is alone. He is lost. He is scared. There is no such thing as an enemyless bullfighting arena in the multitude of memories stored in him. It does not exist. Neither does the novel sense of being powerless, of having the world against him.

That is how I feel, emerging from the subway station at the foot of the World Trade Center, after my prolonged underground ride. The volume of the towers, their size, screams one word at me, etches it into my skin as I pause atop the stairs, holding on to the railing: *Impossible!*

I cannot breathe. Cannot move, talk, think. I am dismayed, my dream dissolved. I feel fear. Glued to the railing, I am an invalid. I stare, I look, I glance, I observe, I watch. My scrutiny yields only

two monoliths, beyond all scale, and carves deeper into me the word: *Impossible!*

Defeated, disgusted, I am about to retreat, but the bold capital U of the towers changes into a powerful horseshoe magnet of gargantuan proportions that draws me nearer its footing.

Avoiding the guards, I trespass onto the plaza, which is still under construction. I reach one of the towers. Facing a corner, I position myself an inch away from the seven-foot-wide metallic face. At my feet, the connection between vertical aluminum panel and horizontal concrete slab is flawless, but surely the wall does not start where I stand. It must surge from the entrails of the earth.

I press my chin against the cold aluminum, forcing my eyes upward, in search of the end of the wall. There is no end. This wall has no top. Instead, it becomes sky—aluminum into azure!

I lie against this narrow strip of unknown land, looking up, until I comprehend: it is a landing field for extraterrestrial vessels. No! A takeoff field: the clouds give it direction—a limitless runway into heaven. It is definitely not man-made, nor of any use to us humans. So uncertain is its length—call it height—and so alien its design, the dreaded word has now infiltrated my heart: *Impossible! Impossible! Impossible!* it pounds. I can no longer breathe.

A very cold chin calls me back to reality. I lower my tired eyes to the ground and glance at the base of the other tower, as if it would be useful to figure the distance between the two corners. It is not. The merest attempt at estimating, the slightest unconscious recording, is shrugged off as an absurd association with some never-to-be-realized dream . . . as an exercise in futility.

I long to flee, but still the colossal magnet controls my destiny. I find myself approaching the other tower, discovering an exit door left ajar, sneaking inside a narrow path, ducking under a "No Trespassing" chain, running up some emergency stairs, jumping inside an elevator, going up, going down, getting lost, avoiding guards. I find a safe staircase and climb as fast as I can, passing floors occupied by offices noisy with activity. As I continue to climb, the offices become silent, then vacant. Then the floors lose their partitions. Now I can see windows all around me; there are no more walls. I am high in the sky. Each floor I climb looks more like a construction site. I bump into construction workers as my body language declares, "What are you looking at? I'm the owner of these buildings!"

I've been running upwards for an hour when I taste the summit's fresh air, seeping through a forest of structural steel. With a little help from heaven, out of breath and unchallenged, I manage to pass my head through an opening to the rooftop.

My tiny staircase pierces the roof near its center. I stay a moment sheltered below the penultimate step, halfway through the trapdoor, lost in contemplation. There is a huge red crane by my side, and behind me an enormous rusty I-beam contraption to support an antenna. Around me spreads the naked platform, a mistake amid the clouds. I step out onto the rooftop. No railing—if I run, I'll finish my course in thin air, changed into a bird. The roof is deserted. Despite its immensity, its exposure on all sides renders it tiny, almost fragile. It's an indestructible aerie, a fortress at the mercy of the next gust.

The city has vanished, the world is no longer in motion, humanity has ceased to exist. There is no notion of "around," no "over there," certainly no "below." The union of altitude and solitude fills me with an arrogant sense of ownership. After all, the sky is my domain.

Unsure this isn't just a dream, yet conscious of my vulnerable position and not wanting to impose unnecessary vibrations from my weight in motion, I tiptoe—carefully, yes—to the corner facing the other tower.

There! Another floating slab! So near, yet a continent apart. And that's when I see the word stretched across the gap between rooftops in all its obscene syllabic obesity: *Im—pos—si—ble!*

16

Moving my head left to right like a child in the first grade, I read it and read it and read it. Then I lean over the edge, ready to climb down the inclined columns to the six-inch ledge eleven feet below that connects the 110th floor with 1,350 feet of verticality, so I can look straight down. I do not. Because that's when it strikes me: teeth clenched, eyes half closed, in horror, in delight, I manage to whisper my first thought (whisper, so the demons won't hear): "I know it's impossible. But I know I'll do it!"

At that instant, the towers become "my towers."

As I run downstairs like a thief, careful to avoid capture, it dawns on me: I had not dared to reach the ledge, had not risked looking down. It was enough to look across.

Once on the street, a new thought: *Impossible, yes, so let's get to work.*

POSITIVE IMPRESSIONS

I am in a huge store buying all the different postcards of the twin towers. (Some fall into my bag by accident.) I could stand here comparing them for hours, but Jim Moore is on time.

I decide to infiltrate the same tower at the same hour as yesterday. My companion is sure we're going to be arrested.

Taking the same haphazard itinerary, running into the same situations, surprise encounters, escapes, and miracles, we emerge with the same success on the rooftop, which is again deserted.

Jim's face whitens as he gazes at the other tower. The altitude has hit him. Or is it the project's magnitude?

I catch him mumbling to himself, "You're insane!"

"Extraordinary!" I whisper, radiant.

Sitting on a beam at the strategic corner, I point at the taunting roof facing me: Jim snaps the shot that will, until walk day, symbolize *le coup*, keep it alive and hold me prisoner of—yes—the insanity *extraordinaire* to which I've willingly shackled myself.

Indulgently following my directions, Jim moves around the roof, taking pictures of construction areas and close-ups of the equipment. Meanwhile, I lean over the flat bar of the upper edge. Again I consider climbing down to the lower ledge, where the sheer aluminum cliff initiates its vertiginous descent.

Yesterday I dared not. Today I must.

ALMIGHTY VOID

It cannot be done all at once. To overpower vertigo—the keeper of the abyss—one must tame it, cautiously.

Brushing aside any thought of climbing down to the lower ledge, I step up onto the flat bar that runs thigh-high along the corner of the roof's upper edge, and begin to balance on it. It's a piece of metal half an inch thick by six inches wide. It feels a bit like a cable under my feet. I manage to hold my balance on one leg for a second or two.

"Jim! Quick!"

A photo is taken. But I did not enjoy this balance. It was somehow faked, timid. I felt overpowered by the sky from all sides. Encouraged nonetheless, I step over the flat bar with extreme caution. I climb along one of the inclined columns, focusing on my hands and feet, until I reach the elevated steel gutter that forms the definite rim of the building. Where the void reigns, almighty. Where the unreachable rampart of the other summit can be seen rising in all its splendor. Oh! I am terrified. It's the towers and me, on a background of clouds, of blue air. Cruel confrontation. The wind, the howling depth prevent me from talking to them, them from hearing me. They are masterful, they rule. I am insignificant. Mid-air battle. I force my unwilling body to lean over, over this . . . this absence of the tangible, this . . . Ah, yes, my mind registers, far, far down, the ground, the streets—but my eyes refuse. Yet I breathe in voluptuously the unknown that eddies below. I keep fighting.

"I have one picture left," announces Jim. In order to look up at him, I must first hold on to the structure, or I chance being pulled into the bottomless canyon.

I notice an old bristleless broom at his feet: "Pass me the broom."

"You sure?"

"Pass me the broom!"

I let go of the column in order to position the broomstick in equilibrium on my forehead. I take my fingers away, and the broom stands freely, balancing in the breeze. For how long, maybe the count of four heartbeats? Then it regains its independence, leaning away. I twist my neck. I bend sideways. The broom and the funambulist together fall slowly into the jaws of the wind.

No!

I resist the fall.

Again I bring the unwilling, awkward prop to the vertical, balance it another second, and quit. I have won. No one will ever know I slipped the tip of my left shoe under the gutter to help hold myself steady during the delicate balance.

It is all too grand down there, up here. I will have to come back, again and again, a hundred, a thousand times. To inhale the altitude, to savor the ever-growing depth, to find myself alone with the towers, nose to nose, before I am capable of challenging them. For the moment, they are so much more solid than I am.

Jim is wary of the time already spent. The sky grows menacing; we wrap it up.

AT 40,000 FEET

As we climb through all shapes of clouds, I press my nose to the window, fascinated, and wait.

The cabin floor is gently brought back to horizontal as the plane attains cruising altitude. I reach for my collection of postcards and the freshly printed photographs, which I review carefully until I doze off.

Suddenly—a geyser—an idea surges and wakes me up: all the equipment needed for the coup is already on the roof! All I have to do is sneak in with a few tools. Feverishly, I spread the pictures on the tiny tray in front of me. That wire over there, wrapped around the crane's winch, will do as a walk-cable. I can link a couple of the chain-hoists scattered around and create a tensioning device. The cable clamps I need, I'll take from these lines here, securing this pylon. There's rope everywhere, enough for making cavalettis, the vibration-reducing guy-lines I'll need to tie to the walk cable. And for a balancing pole, I can use one of those metal pipes over there, why not.

The airline stationery I requested is brought to my seat. It reads, "Air France, *en plein ciel, le* ____." Not bothering to fill in the date, I cover a dozen sheets with frantic notes, sketches, and lists, establishing the first rigging plan. Nothing is left out. I'll need someone to help on my side, and two people for the other tower.

Next, I write Jim a note: "I'll be back in a couple of months to execute the coup."

Done.

JEAN-LOUIS

As soon as I get off the plane, I mail Jim's letter and rush toward the suburb of St.-Germain-en-Laye. I reach an old house, run up five flights of stairs, and bang on the door: "Police, open up!"

No response, but the door slowly opens by itself. As I enter, it slams behind me. Two fingers imitating the barrel of a handgun hit me in the back: "Hands up, freeze!"

That's Jean-Louis.

We were sixteen when his favorite activity, photography, and mine, funambulism, caused us to meet. Unlike other kids, Jean-Louis was encouraging and respectful as he saw me install my first wire and watched me practice between two majestic cedars in the backyard of the local youth hostel. After much observing, he asked if he could take pictures. I asked if he would allow me into his darkroom to observe printmaking. Fascinated by each other's "professions," we became friends.

It was Jean-Louis who threw the ball across the towers at Notre-Dame, helped me rig all night, took pictures of me waiting past dawn, and shared his exclusive reportage of the performance with the world.

My companion from adolescence has barely changed. His tall, broad-shouldered frame still sits upon two solid legs ready for action. His piercing eyes, constantly recording, light a serious face that is nevertheless quick to melt into an engaging smile.

"Go ahead, tell America!" teases Jean-Louis.

"Wait! I have to see if you're still in shape! I don't share my coups with klutzes!" I position a stool in the center of the room, and Jean-Louis ten inches away. "Go for it!"

With no preparation, feet together, Jean-Louis leaps over the obstacle, and lands softly. Then he pulls out an immaculately folded hand-kerchief, opens it, pats the sweat from his forehead, and refolds it meticulously before he buries it in his pocket, deadpan.

"Now we're talking!" I grin, and proceed to describe my fabulous project . . .

Soon Jean-Louis interrupts. "Who are you kidding? Your fabulous project—it's a joke. You don't know what's on the other rooftop. You don't know what time the construction crews start and quit work. You don't even know the distance between the towers! Sure, I'll do the coup with you, but you've got to work things out. And the wind—you thought about the wind?"

"The wind? Yeah. Don't worry. So . . . you're in?"

"Sure."

True, I don't have a plan.

ANNIE

Then Annie resurfaces.

Annie, whom I have not seen for six months.

Annie, who knows me better than anybody.

Annie, who was at my side during my discovery of the wire.

Annie, who encouraged and advised me.

Annie, often withdrawn, occasionally shy or suddenly blooming.

Annie, who listens.

Annie, who does not hesitate to cut through my brilliant discourses with sharp criticisms—causing an immediate rift until the next reconciliation.

Annie, whose large green eyes move me when she looks around, taking in everything.

Annie, who holds me. Our silhouettes are similar: not too tall, not too firm. When we embrace, we look like two kids plotting our next piece of mischief.

At the counter of the brasserie where we rendezvous, Annie leans her elbows on the zinc, creating with her long, thin fingers a sort of woven basket within which she delicately sets her pale face, framed by wavy brown hair.

She's observing me.

Feverishly, I announce my next illegal walk.

Annie listens, entertained. She's obviously proud to have succeeded at last in adopting a distance from me.

She bids me adieu.

I promise, "*À bientôt*," because the coup cannot happen without her support.

"WTC"

Insensible to the passing of time, I browse through bookstores of all persuasions. When permitted, I search the archives of architectural societies. For days, slouched in a plush armchair of the dark, muffled, imposing Bibliothèque Nationale, I dig and probe. I extract all the information Paris is withholding about New York's World Trade Center. As my knowledge of the twin towers grows, so does my collection of magazine stories, newspaper articles, scientific studies, and photos.

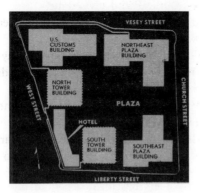

Now Annie joins me, and within two weeks our harvest proves bountiful.

My ever-expanding file soon needs a container; the container needs a title. I transfer three black capitals—Elzevir, I recall—onto the spine of an orange photographic-stock box found in the garbage: the dossier "WTC" is created.

Overnight, I no longer speak of "the twin towers" or "the World Trade Center." Instead, I refer to my idée fixe by the new tongue-snapping acronym WTC.

And each time I open the orange box, the evidence jumps out: the WTC I'm getting to know is a building project soon to be completed—not the three-dimensional, pulsating organism whose steel skeleton I need intimate knowledge of. For that, I must go back.

I must venture again into the belly of the beast.

NEW YORK MAGIC

The moment I set foot on American soil, a somber customs agent singles me out from the line, tells me to drag my suitcase to a table in the corner, and orders, "Open up!"

The first item under scrutiny is a canvas pouch the size of a shoe-box.

The inspector pulls out decks of playing cards—some blank, some made up of fifty-two tens of clubs—fake fingers, double-headed coins, make-believe burning cigarettes with glowing ashes at the tip. Exhausted by a sleepless flight, not in the mood to play the magician, I wait for the old man's question.

No question.

Instead, the officer grabs an ordinary deck and spreads it into an impeccable fan, which he thrusts at my chest, barking, "Take a card, any card!" An amateur illusionist welcomes a fellow criminal to the shores of his future crime. Joyful omen!

A line of passengers has formed behind me, waiting to be

searched. Absorbed by his routine, the prestidigitator merely shrugs and, hardly looking up from the silver dollar he is about to vanish, shouts, "Hey, Jack, take those people, will ya? Don't you see I'm busy here?"

And so it goes—"Do you know this flourish?" "What about this one?" "Oh, can you do that again?"—while above our heads flags of all nations flutter in the air-conditioning . . . or is it the Babelesque brouhaha?

SPY TIME

By dawn, as if waiting for a friend, I stand post outside the revolving doors that give entrance to the cathedral hall of one tower.

Soon the first construction workers appear. I jot down what they wear, the color of their helmets, what tools dangle from their belts, the supplies they carry, the equipment they dolly in.

Then the office workers start arriving. I pay attention to the routes they take. Why do some pack themselves beyond the point of safety into an elevator while other cars remain empty? Why do certain employees detour to a temporary guard booth to flash an I.D. card?

It's now rush hour: the crowd thickens; lines start forming at the newsstand. Like blood in an artery, the flow of human lives keeps pouring through the halls, pulsating: *Stop, go. Stop! Go, go, go!* The sleepy murmur of early arrivals mounts to bustling clamor. There is yelling. There is shouting. Doors slam. People bump into each other. People run. Frequently, someone waves above the sea of heads to greet a fellow employee recognized in the distance.

I spot an imaginary friend about to step into an elevator, "Paul! Paul! Wait!" I run after the phantom, brushing by the guards, stepping on toes. Too late! The doors just close in front of me. Minutes later I try again. "Hey, John! John!" I'm not boarding the elevator. I'm just practicing.

By late morning the site calms down; the crowd dissipates. It's pleasantly quiet.

Finally lunchtime arrives: security personnel relax, businessmen roll up their sleeves and loosen their ties, everyone is hungry, no one cares; the buzz rises to a joyful roar. The multitude is back.

That's when I enter.

Jumping from elevator to elevator, I always manage to reach a higher floor; trying staircase after staircase, I always succeed in ending up on the rooftop—invariably, lunch break ensures it's deserted.

My clandestine visits become daily affairs.

I specialize in lunchtime!

Each attempt makes me smarter at steering clear of the guards, more efficient at dealing with surprise encounters, at avoiding construction foremen. Although I still get lost and get chased, sometimes I feel I'm mapping out the skeleton of an itinerary.

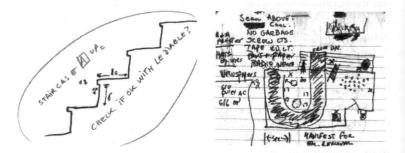

Once on the roof, I proceed with an inventory of the equipment I could use for the rigging. I locate hiding places, I check possible anchor points. Often, Jim Moore joins me, his cameras cautiously recording it all. When our rooftop clamors back to construction racket, we head down to the streets—always an easier exercise than getting to the roof.

In the early afternoon, improvising a disguise, I impersonate a homeless drunk whose territory is an inclined sidewalk by a ramp

I recently discovered: a ramp leading under the towers, a ramp constantly used by delivery vans and the giant trucks of moving companies.

On a tiny pad, I record discreetly the time of entry and exit of each vehicle as well as what's painted on it—a company name, a telephone number, a logo. I note the driver's uniform. I count the passengers. When a police car uses the ramp—which is often, there must be a police station underground—I slouch down, offering less of my vagabond silhouette.

Then it is time to run back to the revolving doors, so as not to miss the exodus of steel workers, electricians, painters, and contractors of all trades, done with their day's work. More observations, more notes.

Soon thereafter I make sure I catch the first businessmen going home. I usually remain until the crowd grows into an out-of-control stampede, until thousands of employees, now tired, now silent, rush out shoulder to shoulder like buffalo fleeing a burning prairie. Actually, they remind me of a scene from *How the West Was Won*.

Sometimes an office worker will turn suddenly and disappear back into the tower, apparently having forgotten something on his desk. Great, I can use that later.

I watch for an hour as the ground vibrates, and then they are gone.

In the evening, I go back. I dare to approach the I.D. desks where visitors must check in; I glance at the logbook when the guard is not looking. I roam around hallways and tunnels, trying not to look suspicious: I must understand how the security works. Why so many different types of guards? How often do the police show up? Some floors stay lit all night—why? Are the offices empty, are people still working up there?

Day after day, again and again, I follow the same routine. And I never get caught.

28

For a long time, I visit only the north tower. It simply doesn't occur to me to spread my scouting trips evenly between the towers. In fact, I don't even realize it is the north tower I keep visiting. It just happens to be the first tower I reach when I come out of my usual subway exit and enter the temporary tunnel that gives access to both towers.

Only later, when I create a map of the area with all the WTC buildings (existing or soon to be built) and the surrounding streets, do I begin to differentiate between the north and south towers, and to refer to them with the architect's original titles: WTC I/tower A (north) and WTC II/tower B (south). And only later still do I learn that the north tower was the first to rise from the ground and the first to reach completion.

FIFTEEN MINUTES IN MID-AIR

"Me? Peter Smith."

I find out that the names written down in the heliport register are kept only to alert the families of crash victims. Fine by me.

Jim, all larded up with color film, makes himself comfortable inside the helicopter while I nail the pilot to the ground. "We'll start with a sweeping pass, high and far away from the towers, so that my photographer gets his establishing shots. Then we'll move a bit closer: I want a profile view of each tower at its full height. After that, I need to hover, exactly centered, above each roof but not too high—I'll tell you. We'll finish with a stationary flight between the two rooftops, right in the middle—"

"Oh, I can't do that. FAA regulations won't allow—"

"Well, then, you'll climb to two thousand feet along the vertical axis marking the center of the space between the two towers, very slowly if you can . . . "

I wanted to bring the aircraft where my wire will hang one day, so that I could record the vision I will have in the middle of my walk. Instead, I will have to content myself with staring down at the two summits from above. It may be that once on the wire between these summits, the distance separating me from the ground will appear less grandiose. That's what I want to believe. But mind and eye are capricious accomplices.

As the machine extracts itself thunderously from the concrete pad, my elation knows no bounds. We climb. We slide, glide, twirl. Visibility is 100 percent.

We dance a farandole around WTC as I laugh with pleasure.

Alas, the pilot does not manage to approach the facades as closely as I want. I complain! He glances out of the corner of his eye at this very demanding tourist. But turbulence caused by the enormous mass of air rushing through the funnel between the towers makes the helicopter vibrate more at each attempt. "Damn currents . . . always at that spot," the pilot mutters.

I know he is absolutely wrong! I am certain my brother the wind softens at times, just to admire a wirewalker passing by; and yes, I'll watch out when he applauds!

Our fifteen minutes are up.

WHAT'S THE DISTANCE?

12.25 meters? No way. A mistake in the conversion of feet to meters? 400 meters? Can't be. In the darkness, did I misplace the decimal point? 200 meters? Shit. I must have forgotten to bring the counter back to zero again.

I have to rent the surveyor's measuring wheel on three different occasions to get it right: 42.06 meters, 138 feet. Definitely.

Ah, finally I can return the stupid machine to the rude, suspicious hardware-store owner on Canal Street and get my extravagant cash deposit back.

Having just learned what I think is the exact distance between the two towers, I add to it my rough estimation of the horizontal distance separating the upper edge from the lower ledge on each roof and come up with, give or take, 50 meters. The space needed to anchor the cable on both sides brings that figure to, hmm . . . 56 meters.

Plus a few meters of unknown.

I decide to call it 60 meters, say 200 feet.

Really, that much?

I.O.

It stands for "isolated occurence."

That's what anthropologists, in their reports, call any atypical finding in the field.

It does not happen often. But today it did. I was rushing up the stairs on the upper floors of the south tower . . . Or was I rushing down? . . . Or was it the north tower? No matter! There was an earthquake.

Well, not really an earthquake—a shake. Inside me.

I stopped and held on to the railing: Was my heart failing me?

Within half a second, the metal steps started quivering beneath my feet. Then, under each of my hands, the rails started vibrating ever so slightly. No, not so slightly. The steps, the railings, my body transmitted their trembling to the stairwell partitions directly around me. And soon, far above me, far under me, the walls, the entire building started shivering, lights flickering.

Through the masonry came the cry of the tower: its steel structure being lengthened and shortened, twisted and squeezed, it let go a plaint of pain. As if guilty of having expressed secret feelings, instantly the tower went totally quiet and totally still.

The swaying of the building must be felt tenfold on the top.

I refuse to imagine what that could do to me on the wire.

31

Look! Jim even took a picture!

The other day, it was windy in the streets.

We arrived on the roof and met a hurricane.

I tried to breathe without a hand covering my nose. I couldn't.

I tried to walk erect without holding on to something. I couldn't.

For fun I embraced a column and let my body be lifted horizontally. Look!

I refuse to think such wind could happen when I walk.

Last week, coming out of the subway, I looked up at my towers and couldn't see past the 78th floors because a thick fog was playing magician, vanishing the upper floors and the roofs for hours.

What if I had been walking the wire at that time?

And went back down and told everyone? And everyone would reply, "Sure you did!"

Usually, an I.O. is not taken too seriously by field scouts, who sometimes bury it in a report, or even omit it.

PHYSICALLY CHALLENGED

A large rusty nail by the plaza's construction site punctures my right foot as I carry out my daily rounds.

I roll on the ground, more in rage than in pain: Aah, how stupid! There goes my research! There goes the entire coup!

I end up in bed with a pachyderm's ankle, thinking about the fog, the swaying, the wind, and everything else that can transform the coup into a failure. I play chess with friends, but in between turns, I see my rooks becoming twin towers, and after each defeat, my excuse is the same: "Oh, I was thinking about WTC!"

After a day and a half of immobility, I still can't put any weight on my foot, but I'm leaving soon for Paris, so, holding on to Ann's shoulder, I hop to the pharmacy at the corner of 96th Street and Madison Avenue to buy a pair of crutches.

Limping and hopping, I drag my sweaty, sorry self back to the towers.

A miracle!

A lame guy on crutches passes everywhere. People hold doors open for him, press elevator buttons for him, ask him all day long, "You okay?"

Yeah, I'm okay, all right!

Without hurrying, I venture into sensitive staircases. Without hiding, I explore dangerous floors. Mistakenly, I open a dozen forbidden doors. Here and there, at strategic places, I sit down to catch my breath, leaning my tired wrists atop propped crutches— no one could invent a more natural attitude—and let my eyes scan the scene. That's how I manage to learn the code above the doorknob of the security gateway that has been resisting me for days: today, several employees punch in 7-7-4-3-5 three feet from me, without so much as a suspicious glance. Whenever a guard surprises me, my infirmity transforms him into a Samaritan who escorts the lost soul all the way to the exit.

The crutches—a trick to remember.

Two days later, when I am able to limp around freely, again I grab the sticks for an improvised premiere: a middle-of-the-night sneak scouting.

It's not easy to get a cab to WTC on 96th Street at 3 a.m. on a rainy Saturday. Two drivers refuse to take me when they learn where I am going—"No one lives down there"—but a third driver does not ask questions, does not say anything, although he stares at me in his rearview mirror at each red light.

The door slams; the taxi speeds away.

I am facing the unfinished commuter tunnel that drills beneath the construction site to reach the underground entrance to both towers. In the rain and dimness it looks like a gigantic black mouth. At my back, a freezing draft whirls across the deserted avenue. Above me, the March wind howls. The towers, mostly dark—how rare—loom before me like a vampire's castle. My trembling silhouette proceeds through the tunnel.

Through the glass panels of the north tower's lobby, I can see the guard at his desk, leaning half asleep on the logbook I know well.

I pace back and forth in the shadows for an hour, drenched and frozen, before I decide to risk the wolf's den.

I hobble through the revolving glass door, reach the desk, lean my crutches against it, nonchalantly pick up the ballpoint pen, and copy the last entry. I give the guard a little wave and direct myself, light-footed, toward the nearest elevator.

Shit! My crutches!

I turn about with a smile, hop back to the desk, pick up the crutches, and disappear like a true handicapped man.

The guard does not react.

Several times during the night, I have to run back downstairs to retrieve the crutches forgotten on the floor where I was—oh so successfully—scribbling my spy plans.

AN ARGUMENT, A FRESCO, A FRIEND

The day before my departure, Jim comes up into the south tower with me. We climb the stairs silently, so as not to attract the attention of the sentinels stationed on the 44th and 78th skylobby landings. At some point we hear a guard descending quickly toward us, walkie-talkie blasting. We have no time to retreat, no place to hide. My reflex is to test my two-people-passing-in-front-of-someone-whose-job-it-is-to-arrest-them hypothesis, which states: Do not slow down. Disregard the hostile presence to the point of

not acknowledging it—bumping is allowed. Draw your accomplice
into a mammoth festival of laughter—tears in your eyes, as out of
control and loud as possible: if you're good, the enemy may join in.
Conversely, engage your co-conspirator in a verbal battle in apparent full swing, each of you roaring your differences on the subject
at hand, spit flying, gesticulating angrily; if you act your parts well,
your true antagonist may step aside to let you pass.

With no time to warn Jim, I go for the loud argument:

"What the hell do you mean, Tuesday? You told Gérard
Tuesday? Are you crazy? Everything is arranged for Wednesday!
You're such an idiot! You really said Tuesday? Answer me!"

"Tu-tuesday?" stutters Jim. But immediately he gets it and
jumps into the improvisation.

Screaming at each other, we pass.

Closer to the roof, before we reach the floors still under construction, we give ourselves a well-deserved break to celebrate our
victory, dry the sweat from our foreheads, and gather our

thoughts. I pull out a black permanent marker and draw the facade of a gothic cathedral on the plaster wall of the stairwell, at eye level. Between the two towers, I add a line with a wirewalker on it and, underneath, an inscription: NOTRE DAME, 26 JUIN 1971. Under that, and at the same scale—therefore much larger—I draw a steel arch bridge with a wirewalker between the pylons: SYDNEY HARBOUR BRIDGE, 3 JUIN 1973. At the bottom, I sketch the twin towers of my dream and write WORLD TRADE CENTER, with a bold question mark instead of a date.

I enclose the three drawings in a single oval frame, so they appear as an ensemble, which I sign quite legibly, PHILIPPE PETIT.

Unbeknownst to me, this romantic fresco will almost kill the coup.

On the roof, Jim quickly takes the shots that are missing from my collection and rushes back down to the lab so I'll have the slides before my flight tomorrow. On his way down, he adds to the fresco a misspelled but loving "goodbye Phillipe."

What a pity my new friend, who has been so helpful, encouraging, and enthusiastic, who has taken great pictures instrumental to the coup, refuses to be part of the rigging crew on D day. I tried to convince him, to no avail. He will give all the help I want in and around the towers, but not up there on the day of the coup.

He has his reasons.

I stay for hours at the top, making a final technical inspection. Jean-Louis's intuition is confirmed: the equipment I need for a safe rigging can't be chosen from what clutters the roofs. I'll have to bring my own gear.

My work is interrupted regularly by prolonged stares at the other roof, by forgetful gazes at the void.

Suspended between the tangible and the ephemeral, I find myself pondering: Would anyone but a crazed bicephalous being, half engineer, half poet, willingly shackle himself to a venture of such magnitude? I am prisoner of my dream.

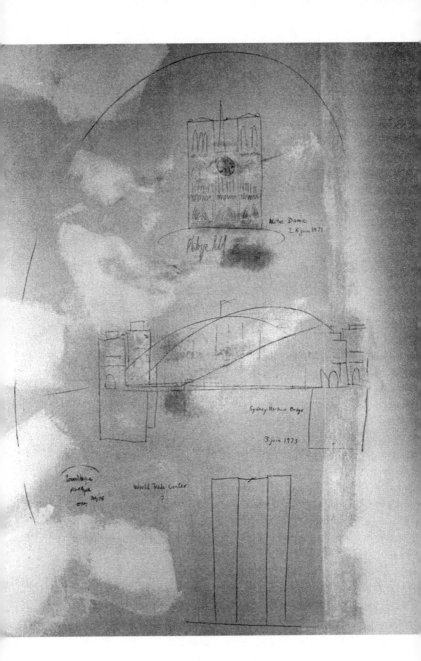

Notre Dame
26 juin 1971

Sydney Harbour Bridge

3 juin 1973

World Trade Center

Compared to the ad-lib observations and the bits of knowledge I gathered during my first visit to America, the intelligence I have recently collected, along with all the sketches, measurements, and photographs, constitutes a professional study addressing most of the project's concerns. Or so I convince myself.

Everything finds its place inside a thin, spiral-bound high school notebook, 8½ by 11 inches, its title written in longhand: "WTC Organization."

Nothing fancy. A tool.

The first WTC *cahier* is born. And thickens.

For example, today I enter:

Saturday, March 9, 1974. Back to Paris.

If my prediction is correct, the coup should happen mid-June, say Sunday, June 16. The next day in case of bad weather.

GALLOPING IN EUROPE

Ill-fated.

That's how I feel after I miss my flight because it fails to appear on the electronic screen at the airport. The next plane to Paris is tomorrow. I vehemently demand a three-star hotel; I'm given a deck chair in an abandoned back room supposedly reserved for flight attendants. In the turmoil, I realize, I left my pocketbook in front of the screen. I run back: of course it's gone. I don't care about the money, but it was full of notes and ideas waiting to be copied into the WTC cahier. I search frantically for hours and interrogate virtually every human being in the terminal, then go back to my den and fall asleep in despair. In the middle of the night, a black giant in uniform points his flashlight, then his stick at me when I refuse to follow his order to leave. He states that I have no right to be in this part of the airport. I claim I do. He points his gun at me. I smile. "If you want me out of here, you'll have to kill me, then drag the body."

The giant leaves.

To me, this disastrous departure day is an omen.

I find a telephone, hide under a desk, and spend most of the night figuring out the code to obtain an outside line. I call Ann and share with her my misfortune in the most disheartened terms. "Anyway," I conclude, "in a few months I'll be dead."

During the flight the next day, I study Jim's slides. Bits of plan escape from bits of film. Hope returns. I end up covering pages of the WTC *cahier* with my beloved lists and schedules.

Here is the best one:

PARIS: Jean-Louis/final plans and dates
GERMANY: Francis/money
PARIS: build model/find crew/how to pass the cable?
BLOIS: Omankowsky/rigging problems
VARY: rehearsing/equipment/preparations
BACK TO NEW YORK!

Upon landing, I go see Jean-Louis. With pride, I unpack my photos, the *cahier*, my information, my perfect knowledge of the towers. It doesn't produce the effect I expected. Yes, the pictures from the helicopter impress him, yes, he salutes my promenading at length inside both towers, but he still doesn't find any answers to his essential questions concerning the coup.

Why won't Jean-Louis share my enthusiasm?

The next day, I go to meet Francis, who is juggling in a circus somewhere in Germany.

Why do I decide to hitchhike, with no money and no luggage, when my foot is not yet healed and I am the owner of a truck in perfect working order? And why, after only an hour of waiting at the highway entrance, do I give up on signaling the passing cars, and begin to walk toward Germany? Have I gone insane?

No. I'm thirsty for freedom, for adventure.

I walk for miles and miles on French, on German asphalt, in the rain, belting songs, barefoot when my wound wakes up. I sleep in barns. I pick up leftover bread in train station cafeterias. Far away I see the cathedral of Frankfurt. I reach the white-and-green big top of Circus Sarrasani. I lift the canvas.

Francis is rehearsing the six hoops. He asks, "Why are you here? Why didn't you call?"

With machine-gun delivery, I explain, "I-just-came-back-from-New-York-I-rented-a-helicopter-I-sneaked-into-the-towers-hundreds-of-times-I-know-them-by-heart-I-have-thousands-of-photographs-dozens-of-friends-to-help-me-I'm-about-to-build-a-model-of-the-two-roofs-I'm-going-rehearsing-in-the-country-I-must-buy-equipment-and-airline-tickets-to-bring-the-crew-to-New-York-we-must-rent-an-apartment-and-eat-during-the-entire-preparation . . . "

Out of breath, I conclude, "I came . . . I need money!"

Francis backs up, startled. "But, Philippe, why didn't you call? I can't give you any money today. Come back next week."

"I'll be back!"

Back to rue Laplace. With my pictures and sketches as references, I help Phil, the model maker, build a scale wooden replica of the two roofs and the three floors below. The baseboard is so large it occupies the whole width of the broom closet I call home, balancing between the tiny woodworking bench and the gutted piano I use as a desk. But everything is glued, too late for changes.

I resign myself to crawling under the model to get to the door or go to bed. I am reminded of Marie-Antoinette, in her cell at the Conciergerie—or was it the Bastille?—waiting to be beheaded: every time she was called for interrogation, she had to come out through a low postern, which forced her to bow to the waiting magistrates. She solved that problem by walking out with her torso upright on acutely bent legs.

I can't do that, the model is too low. So I bow to WTC twenty times a day.

The next decision concerns cavalettis; how many to use and how far apart to space them. The questions of where to attach them and how to keep them tight will come later.

To the model, I quickly add a high wire of red sewing thread, and to the wire, two pairs of blue-thread cavalettis. These two ropes ride the walk cable, creating four legs inclined toward the ground; their purpose is to reduce the vibrations on the wire. Because they create an area of steadiness, because they reduce the emptiness by constructing a three-dimensional shape in the void, because they offer an additional object of visual focus, and because the wirewalker feels he can hold on to them in case of trouble, the places where the cavaletti ropes connect with the cable always represent a safe haven. The wise rigger of high wires spaces his cavalettis prudently.

I try various intervals on the model but have difficulty appreciating the distances on such a small scale, so I grab a piece of chalk and, bending under the model, rush outside.

At the place du Panthéon, I draw a line on the pavement 60 meters long. I mark several different cavaletti arrangements, each time trying the wire by slowly walking its length, focusing on the anchor point far ahead and carrying an immense, invisible balancing pole . . .

"Asshole!"

"What the fuck are you doing?"

"Are you nuts?"

Three angry motorists in succession nearly run me over. In my excitement, I was not fully aware that I had drawn the wire in the middle of a curve in the road, and that darkness had already fallen upon Paris.

What is this? A crumpled note taped to my mailbox reads, "Hi Philippe!" It's signed "Le cheval." The mystery repeats itself three days in a row. Then there is a knock on the door. Ah, my friend Mark from Australia! Of course: "the horse." I had forgotten how, during the night of illegal rigging on the bridge, I had jumped on his back despite his full load of equipment and screamed "Charge!" and he had dashed ahead, galloping.

I tell the shaggy, smiling young giant about my new clandestine project.

An hour later, my Australian accomplice says yes to WTC.

I spend most of my time tying threads of different colors to the model, vainly trying to figure out where to anchor the wire, how many cavalettis are needed, and where to tie them. Annie has to drag me out to eat, force me to sleep. As my frustration grows, she keeps repeating, "Go ask Omankowsky."

Professor Rudy Omankowsky, Sr.—"Papa Rudy," creator and director of the illustrious Czechoslovakian troupe of wirewalkers Les Diables Blancs—has been my mentor, rigging-wise, all along. Already several of his expensive secrets (yes, in the beginning I had to buy them!) have saved my life. There's no one better to quickly set a cable between two mountains, over a lake, or across a city, but Omankowsky knows nothing about swaying skyscrapers, doesn't believe in finely tuned rigging, and hates engineers.

Jean-Louis comes to look at the model. He examines my forest of threads.

"So, you figured out how to pass the cable!"

Shit, he's right! Before the cable can be anchored, or guy-lined with cavalettis, it must be passed across the void. And in order to pull across the heavy cable, first a thin light line must be set between the towers, followed by thicker and stronger ropes, and ultimately the cable.

How to get a fishing line across? In the dark. Quickly. Without noise. Without being seen. Without failure.

We start to brainstorm.

What about hitting a tennis ball with a racket or a golf ball with a club, or kicking a soccer ball? Sure, but with some leeway on both the transmitter's and the receiver's sides, to land the object not on the edge of the building but in the middle of the roof, the distance becomes almost 100 meters, 300 feet—too great to be that sure, that accurate. Plus there's the drag of the line . . .

"What about a bow and arrow?" suggests Jean-Louis.

"And why not a boomerang while you're at it? Ridiculous!" I snap.

I propose a fly-fishing rod, with a lead weight instead of a hook. A trap-shooting machine flinging a clay pigeon. Even two ballast-terminated ropes, one swaying from each roof, drawn to connect in the middle by magnets!

Jean-Louis goes from the bow to the crossbow to the harpoon gun.

Why not a cannon? I ask. Why not a launching ramp complete with radio-guided rocket? Oh, that's it: an airplane! One of those miniature models operated by remote control.

We run to the bottom of rue de la Montagne Ste. Geneviève, where there is a shop specializing in such things. I am distracted by the helicopters in the window. We'll tie the fishing line to the skid, I tell Jean-Louis, guide the chopper up, straight, down, and we're done. Or, we'll do it from the ground, unnoticed, then return the next day to find the fishing line already across, waiting for us. We could also use the helicopter as a getaway vehicle for

Jean-Louis's film—send it to a nearby rooftop before the cops can confiscate it. . . . But Jean-Louis is already inside the store, so I follow.

This is no toy shop—it's for serious model makers. A very professional man in a white lab smock asks us questions. It is clear he first suspects us of wanting to smuggle drugs across the border. When he understands that our objective is to pass a fishing line between two buildings, he gives us a smile of pity and lectures us on the difficulties of radio-guiding model airplanes. He estimates it would take us a year or two to master the beginner's model. "Add to that a couple of years if you wish to control the helicopter."

Add to that, I'm completely uninterested, I say to myself, having just heard a salesman at the other end of the store demonstrating how to start an engine: these mini-motors make more racket than the buses outside. So much for stealth.

Another precious hour lost.

Did I mention *Metropolis?*

Still looking to update my technical file on WTC, with Annie posing as my secretary I wangle a meeting with an architectural publisher to pitch an article on the twin towers, complete with an interview of the workers at the top.

I'm not in the mood. My acting is at its worst. Rather than throw me out, the lady behind the desk, to get rid of me and out of compassion for the loser I am, kindly gives me some sort of letter of introduction—just a line scribbled on a large bristol card imprinted with her company's logo.

At home, I attempt to transform this not very useful document into a better one, adding text and substituting my own phone number.

The result is less than acceptable.

I'm furious. Another precious day lost.

By now, not only friends but also friends of friends know my secret. An air mail envelope from Argentina lands in my mailbox. It contains a message written in purple ink on onionskin stationery:

Philippe,
I was thinking about this idea you have. Have you given some thought to the high-velocity winds systematically generated by very tall structures?
I'm sure there are some books to be found on the subject.
Yours,
Antoine

Another question also prevents me from sleeping lately. In search of answers, I go engineer-hunting. Since disagreement seems to be the pastime of that profession, I expect to collect multiple opinions, but the responses are disconcertingly similar:

"Oh, it's pretty simple"—here all of them clear their throats—"the towers have been designed to sway, and it's not your tiny cable"—here their tone shows technical disdain—"that will prevent them from doing so. A violent draft or a sudden change of temperature will force the entire structural-steel skeleton alternately to expand and contract, a phenomenon known as harmonic oscillation. The tension in the wire-rope will go instantly from three to three thousand tons. The whole thing will explode, and you with it."

How I would have loved them to differ!

Even Alain, the world's youngest airline pilot, the sensational acrobatic flyer who last year coaxed me into joining him for an unforgettable demonstration of *voltige*, sneaking his Stampe under telephone wires along deserted country roads; Alain, whose extreme cold-bloodedness and impeccable rigor of judgment I admire; Alain, who already suspects my new coup and whom I invite to the Vietnamese restaurant on rue Laplace; even he tells me the project contains too many unknowns.

"You're on your way to getting really screwed!" he says, and, setting his chopsticks aside, he explains with his hands how turbulence, air vacuums, and whirlpools form in the vicinity of towers.

Undaunted, I ask him if he'll help with the rigging.

"Listen," he says. "If you need me on such and such a day, at such and such an hour, and my job is clearly defined, I'll be there if I possibly can. But right now you're completely dreaming. All that you're telling me—the helicopter, the model, the pictures, the friends—it's cute, but you've got nothing solid. And for me to be there, it's gotta be rock-solid."

Ouch! Worse than Jean-Louis.

PAPA RUDY

"Let's go see Omankowsky!" I bark to Annie, as if it were my idea. I've just spent another frustrating morning with the model, tying and untying colored threads.

As we drive away from Paris, my mood lightens. Passing Blois, I find myself singing Russian songs. Annie reminds me I had better gather my thoughts: I have a list of rigging questions for Omankowsky, and it's never easy to get straight answers from him. I practice aloud, with Annie playing a distracted, unfocused, anecdote-spewing Papa Rudy.

"Make a right!" she screams when I almost miss the intersection.

We arrive at dusk at the edge of a tiny wine-growing village. I park the truck in front of a red portal protecting a two-story brick pavilion surrounded by thick ivy. Practice wires can be seen in the garden, but the house seems asleep; the shutters are closed, all is quiet. I honk, and instantly, as if it were a surprise party, a joyful, almost dancing group appears from behind the residence. Here comes Papa Rudy, a diminutive yet savagely strong man in a Bavarian jacket

and short-sleeve shirt with a silver bolo at the collar. His round face displays a wide smile, but his teeth are clenched and his mouth is shut—how does he do that? Between fingers so thick there is no way his fist can close, he delicately holds, as a mother gorilla would her newborn, a golden cigarette holder. As he approaches, three playful dogs bounce off him so exuberantly they would prevent any other human being from walking straight.

"Holla! Mister Brown! Anita!" greets the old performer, kissing us each six times and squinting merrily.

Inside, the frail yet authoritative Mrs. Omankowsky is finishing her preparation of the mandatory *Goulash mit Knedliky* I've learned to appreciate. As usual, the house is overheated, overdecorated with pictures of their wirewalker children and kitsch from all over the world, and overloud with four television sets blasting, three dogs barking, two cats fighting, and the loud, disrespectful squawking of a cockatoo Papa Rudy has taught to repeat insults in six languages.

There's no way to address Omankowsky during dinner: he has to tell me about the health problems of Circus Knie's hippopotamus. After dinner is no good either. Snifter in hand, we must play chess in the way I hate: talking, talking, talking. Whenever I bring up the subject of WTC, Papa Rudy is reminded of another circus story to share.

I try until three in the morning. And I thought I was tenacious!

Determined to corner the old man tomorrow, I fall asleep with Annie, under a rack of poisoned arrows framed by a pair of shrunken human heads.

At 6 a.m., Papa Rudy bounds into our room without knocking, wearing a poncho and a sombrero, and serenades us with Mexican love songs on his guitar.

By noon, I succeed in showing the model to Papa Rudy and start asking questions. With hardly a look at the wire and cavalettis, he makes faces at Annie and asks, "Why is Philippe in such a bad mood?" But for this circus veteran, a glance at the model is all he needs. He has instantly understood all my rigging problems, computed all the parameters in his head, and arrived at the solutions. He shares them with me at last only because he is alarmed to see me so white, teeth clenched, trembling with frustration and on the edge of tears. And maybe because Annie's supplicating eyes have not let go of his for quite some time.

In less than five minutes, I have all my answers, including many that I disagree with, and the model is damaged—because you can't tell Papa Rudy, "Don't touch!"

When I bring up wind turbulence and structural swaying, he becomes violent: "Nobody knows! Nobody knows!"

"But I talked with some engineers who—"

"Engineers! A bunch of numskulls! They know nothing!" he roars, striking the oak table with his enormous fist. I hear a crushing noise—his knuckles, or the table?

Suddenly, he pulls me to the salon. He wants to talk to me in private, he has an idea. He whispers to me: On the wire I must install a little metal carabiner linked by a very thin wire to a safety belt concealed under my costume. "Nobody will notice at such height."

I try to dismiss the notion on practical grounds—the ring will get stuck where the cavalettis are tied to the cable. Papa Rudy gets almost angry: "Come on! Are you a wirewalker or are you not a wirewalker? You just kneel there, people will think you are saluting. You unhook the damn ring and you clip it on the other side of the cavaletti, come on!"

In the gentlest manner, I explain to my friend, daredevil of the old circus tradition, how our wires are different, how mine is a theater stage, a canvas on which to paint poetry. About the safety belt, I conclude, "I cannot, I never will . . . do that." Am I speaking another language?

Papa Rudy holds my hand and looks at me with brimming eyes. "Oh, but don't think I can't understand. I know. You want to do something . . . something . . . something beautiful, you!"

Another one who thinks I'm going to die. Except this time it's a wire-walker; he knows.

As Annie and I are departing, Papa Rudy disappears and quickly returns.

"In America, you have something to measure with?"

Without waiting for a reply, he places in my hands an antique leather-bound 50-meter cloth measuring tape, embossed in gold with his grandfather's initials.

"Here, it's a gift, don't lose it."

The old man and his wife insist on waving goodbye at the truck, and they keep waving even after it passes the hill. It's a family tradition. It is how, each year, they send their children off on world circus tours, not entirely sure of seeing them all alive again.

VARY

Blois to Vary, two hundred kilometers.

I know the itinerary like I know my cable: Romorantin. Vierzon. Bourges. Nevers. St.-Pierre-Le-Moutier.

We'll be at Vary before dusk.

Annie is joyful. Omankowsky's advice has somewhat reassured her. I continue to believe that the towers may sway, that the wind may take me out. And I'm still worked up about my unresolved argument with the old master: he says the cavaletti ropes should be tied at the same level as the cable, it's simpler and faster. So what if, during the walk, I have to lift my balancing pole here and there, to avoid hitting the ropes? This idea is unacceptable to me;

it would make the walk inelegant, circuslike. I want traditional cavalettis that slant down from the cable. But where to anchor the ropes on the windowless buildings?

"*Waaaatch it!*" screams Annie, as I swerve to avoid a head-on collision with a sixteen-wheeler.

Concealed in the muddiest countryside imaginable, the hamlet of Vary appears, awaiting its daily rain. The cows start a concert of welcome as we turn down the long dirt road leading to the Castle—that's how the local farmers refer to the large estate my parents intend to sell.

Nothing has changed.

The hundred-foot spruce continues to grow a short distance from the steps of the Big House, a comfortable eighteenth-century mansion with yellow walls, a steep slate roof, and pretentious pinnacles. The Big House is off-limits to me.

Leaning against it, as if to take its place, is a smaller, shorter, much older structure with grapevine fissuring its roughcast facade and handmade tiles in countless shades of red covering a misshapen roof. This tiny mildewed dwelling, with its post-and-beam oak attic where I used to play hide and seek, its single bedroom and adjoining quarters, its lack of running water, is my domain, all that I'm allowed until further notice. And I cherish it.

It was here that I spent a winter writing my *Treatise on the High Wire*, constantly throwing logs at the fireplace. It was on these grounds nine years ago that I installed my first hemp rope between two trees and fought alone, all summer long, for the art of balance. It was across the big meadow that, much later, I stretched my first long practice cable, nine feet off the ground—the Hundred Meters. It still hangs there, sagging alarmingly low to the dung-covered field.

"Quick! No time!"

Constantly talking to myself, I feverishly set up headquarters for the WTC operation while Annie opens the house.

I take the bedroom for Annie and myself and in the living room make a pile of all the old mattresses, pillows, and blankets I can find for the numerous visitors I'm expecting.

I cover the walls with rigging plans, views of the twin towers, and maps of Manhattan. I pin schedules and lists of equipment all over the kitchen in such a way that it's not possible to open all the cabinets. I set the WTC model on the dining table, announcing, "We'll eat on the floor!"

Annie knows better than to intervene.

"Let's go, let's go!" I croon like a rooster every morning at 6 a.m.

On a piece of plywood I paint the words WORLD TRADE CENTER ASSOCIATION, with a large red arrow underneath. I add a silhouette of my towers, a wire, and a wirewalker. Then I nail it to a stake and run to plant the sign at the turnoff for Vary.

I straighten the two Xs supporting the Hundred Meters, wipe the cable, tension it to 5 tons, and throw six cavaletti ropes on it. That's a day's work. Next, I drag out of the barn the "circus installation": two masts 20 feet high supporting a 30-foot cable, all disassembled and rusty. I struggle with the equipment, repairing, scraping, painting all day, forgetting to eat. Wielding a twenty-pound sledgehammer, I'm about to drive the first of twenty-five three-foot steel stakes necessary to anchor the installation, determined to erect it before dark, when Annie breaks in: "You're crazy! It's absurd to kill yourself, rigging the installation alone! In two days, Mark will be here to help you. Instead, you should be practicing the Hundred Meters, getting stronger, making the new balancing pole, preparing your agenda with Jean-Louis—if not, you'll end up arguing with him again . . ."

She's right.

Angered by my own stupidity, I hammer the heavy stake all the way down to the neck and move on to something else.

"*Allo*? Good morning. I'm calling to find out the maximum permissible length for a cylindrical package to be checked as baggage on a flight to New York . . . When am I flying? That's irrelevant, I just— . . . How long is my package? I don't have a package yet. I'm making one. And I wanted to know how long it— . . . Excuse me? Call you when I am finished making the package? No, but you don't understand, I— Wait! Wait!"

I spend the afternoon on the phone, reaching all sorts of offices in every airport of the Paris region, and net—along with insults, hang-ups, and endless discussions—fifteen different answers.

I calculate the mean of all the dimensions I've been quoted and start to make the WTC balancing pole. To fight the wind and to reinforce the illusion that my life is not at stake, it has to be much longer and much heavier than all my previous poles, so it will measure 8 meters long and weigh 25 kilograms. It will break down into four sections, forming a cylindrical package 2.5 meters long, 8.2 feet.

For a full day, I saw, file, weld, hammer, and drill. I paint the finished balancing pole flat black, not only to render it visible in the whitish sky, but to underscore the link between the street-juggler and the funambulist. In my chalk circle on the sidewalk, I always appear dressed in black. Yesterday, in the middle of the night, I decided: I will appear all in black on the wire between my towers.

It's raining.

I don't have enough hours in the day. Not only do I refuse to eat, I start using my nights to sort things out. I don't really sleep: I think in my sleep. In addition to working the Hundred Meters at dawn every day—a grueling exercise—I'm organizing everything. And I'm not good at it.

It keeps raining.

I must get invitation letters from Jim Moore for Jean-Louis, Mark, and me, to facilitate our getting visas long enough to prepare the coup.

The crew has to be reconfigured: two friends have given up already. Mark had the brilliant idea of asking Paul, the other Australian accomplice from Sydney, a young architecture student who is currently in London. I must write to him immediately.

I need to follow Jean-Louis's progress with the bow and arrow. He's coming in three days; we'll practice shooting the fishing line across. If the bow doesn't work, what will?

I call Francis. He has the money. When can I come?

I spend countless sessions with the model, sorting out the remaining technical problems and torturously listing the possible solutions. At times, exhausted, I wonder if Jean-Louis is right: maybe I don't know enough of what I'm supposed to know.

I call Omankowsky for advice, but it's worse on the phone than in person, and we end up yelling at each other.

What about the rest of the equipment? I go buy things. I go make things. It's endless.

Madly, I surround myself with more sketches, more plans, more lists, more schedules, bringing on a Kafkaesque state of asphyxia.

And it's raining.

As if life were not complicated enough, a film crew—friends of friends—is coming to shoot our preparations in 16mm with sound. I've been arguing with the director, Yves, about a contract for a month already. He's calling every five minutes.

It's still raining.

Philippe works with the model – *a still from the 16mm film*

Loud honking at the gate.

It's Mark and his Australian girlfriend, Woose, in a green mini-van held together with gaffer's tape. I give them a calm five-minute tour of the property before I throw work gloves at Mark.

With that extra pair of very fast and very practical hands, and with Annie's help organizing things—which for once I accept—the days find the hours they had lost.

The circus installation is up. I'm on the wire half of the day, happy.

It's stopped raining.

This morning the sky is ready to spit at us.

With a shower of sand, tires screeching, Jean-Louis slides his immaculate white coupé to a halt, almost hitting the front step. I run out with Papa Rudy's measuring tape to check the distance between the bumper and the stone: 15 centimeters.

As Jean-Louis helps his Japanese girlfriend, Setsuko, out of the car, the sky turns black, and suddenly hail the size of quail eggs falls on us with a biblical vengeance.

"Well, when you bring bad weather, you don't do things halfway!" I say.

"Actually, it was snow I was aiming for," deadpans Jean-Louis.

Mark and Woose, Jean-Louis and Setsuko, Philippe and Annie—the house reverberates with international laughter and jokes no one entirely gets.

I make everyone sit around the model, and for the first time I present the coup in its full scope, primarily addressing Jean-Louis.

I quickly grow irritated, at first by the constant joking inter-ruptions from the group, and then by the dawning realization that my presentation is in fact a lengthy exposé of the coup's unsolved problems. I raise my voice, I speak faster to conceal the weaknesses of the project, but I can tell from Jean-Louis's silence that he feels betrayed. The operation I have portrayed as almost ready to go is still a bag of loose ends. And just as I am on the verge of engaging him in a productive exchange, the movie crew enters, camera rolling.

Instantly, Jean-Louis pulls back, frowning. I pick a fight with Yves—the contract again—that continues far into the evening and sets Jean-Louis sulking by the fireplace. When he finally explodes—"It's the film or the coup!"—I shift my wrath to him, and we argue bitterly about ways to sneak into WTC until Annie, who has further enraged me by taking sides with Jean-Louis, throws me out of the living room at 3 a.m.

Everyone goes to sleep without saying good night.

How could I have noticed that, in a dark corner by the chimney, Mark was following every aspect of the technical discussion and analyzing the options?

We breakfast quietly and without joy, but Yves films us.

Suddenly Mark breaks the silence. He has an idea about where to anchor the cavalettis, which he shows me on the model: "You see, if you put this here . . . and this here . . . then you . . . " Still in a foul mood, I begin to tear apart his idea, until the genius of what he suggests dawns on me. Everyone crowds around as Mark once again proudly demonstrates his discovery.

Feverishly, I clear the model of all its threads. I glue a new red wire from tower to tower, not on the midpoint of the lower ledge of the building as before, but this time at the corner of the upper edge. Perpendicular to the wire and at even intervals, I lay two blue cavaletti ropes, fixing each intersection with a drop of glue. Then I tie their four extremities, not to the rooftops but to the ledge 11 feet, 3 inches below, where it is so frightening to stand.

Seen from above, the geometry looks asymmetrical, but in profile it's the best configuration, allowing the cavaletti ropes to slant down slightly from the wire, a compromise between Papa Rudy's horizontal solution and Mark's vertical one.

Everyone applauds and shouts congratulations; Jean-Louis and I wrestle Mark to the floor.

Yves misses shooting the scene, of course.

The weather continues to mimic the group's mood: the sun is shining. We all rush out to the big meadow.

On the tall grass, with wooden stakes and yellow polypropylene ropes, I set the exact perimeters of the two towers facing each other corner to corner, 138 feet apart. Everyone helps.

"Okay, everybody, behind Jean-Louis!" I order, as my friend prepares his bow and arrow.

Jean-Louis picks up a plank he has brought along. Two nails are already half driven into it, three feet apart, and he proceeds to wrap a very long piece of twine around and around the nails, keeping it tight. When he has only a foot of twine left, he swiftly knots a series of clove-hitches at both ends. Then he pulls out the nails, releasing a perfectly made traditional bowstring.

I am impressed. "Where did you learn that?"

Without missing a beat, and without pausing as he hooks the string to the bow, forcing it into a majestic curve, Jean-Louis whispers, "Yes, well, some people do their homework!" Then he takes aim from the "north tower" and hits the center of the "south tower": a bull's-eye. (He boasts that he's been practicing for days, aiming at old ladies in the castle gardens at St.-Germain-en-Laye.)

By happy accident, Yves gets it on film.

But when we tie the 300-foot fishing line to a minuscule hole drilled behind the arrow's feathering, the exercise turns disastrous. After ten minutes of carefully arranging the line in a zigzag behind him, Jean-Louis silences us, takes a deep breath, concentrates, aims, draws, and shoots. And the arrow falls . . . at his feet. That is not on film.

I can't help crowing, "See, I told you it would never work!"

We stay well past lunchtime, trying countless improvements, arguing all the while. Winding the line around a spool that turns freely on a handheld pencil gives a much better result, but still the dead weight of the line makes Jean-Louis undershoot his mark by half.

Once more, Mark saves the day. Borrowing from an ancient fishing technique of his country, he breaks off one of the spool's flanges and sands it smooth. The line can fly off freely in the axis of the pencil. The next attempt is almost a hit. With practice and minor improvements, Jean-Louis should have no problem.

Amid the applause, I yell, "I knew all along the bow and arrow was the solution!" and Jean-Louis laughingly throws me to the ground.

Mark holds the improvised spool as Jean-Louis prepares to shoot –
a still from the 16 mm film

After a delicious salad fresh from the farm's garden and Annie's *mousse au chocolat*, I drag the group outdoors again, ignoring their pleas for a nap.

I start with the circus installation. Accompanied by Nino Rota's music from the scratchy record-player, I perform a brief high wire anthology that includes, in addition to my distinctive walks, the bicycle, the unicycle, the chair, juggling, and somersaults. I reach the ground by walking down the slant wire without balancing pole. "Bravo!" shout my friends.

An appetizer.

Without taking a break, I run to the Hundred Meters, climb on the departure X, grab the waiting pole, and start walking. The cable being properly guy-lined by four well-tightened cavalettis, I reach the arrival X without once stopping.

It takes me only three minutes.

I climb down and impatiently start removing all the cavalettis.

A moment later, I'm back on a naked wire that is free to oscillate.

I grab the pole. I walk. After twenty feet, the cable begins to vibrate. I slow down.

As I progress, the undulations amplify. By midwire, the cable dances an agitated jig. I pause after each step, but keep going. I pass the dreaded middle, even though the out-of-control cable tells me to stop. Anchored to the wire by my toes, riveted to the arrival X by my eyes, I stand there fighting waves two feet high, three-foot lateral swaying, and the jerky, invisible but very palpable rolling of a wire gone berserk.

Yves is filming from a tripod, although the cable is moving so violently that I keep disappearing from the frame.

I let myself be carried in all directions, make myself one with the wire, dead weight, not even breathing. The cable calms down, and soon I am able to resume walking, one step at a time, until eventually, exhausted, elated, I conclude the crossing.

But that's not it.

Ignoring the congratulations of my friends, I shout, "We have barely enough time, help me!" and direct them to replace the four cavalettis on the cable, which I then feverishly retighten.

"Stay close to me!"

I jump back on the wire. I walk firmly to the middle and wait. A few feet behind me, the group gathers under the wire.

"Quick, loosen the tension on the cavalettis, starting with the closest one!"

"Done!" yells Jean-Louis.

The cable starts dancing again, in an even more brutal, erratic way than before; this time, instead of swinging freely, it's carrying the loose cavaletti ropes.

I take the punishment.

"Okay, now move the ropes! Come on, move the ropes! Make them shake!"

First Jean-Louis, then Mark, then everyone gently shakes the ropes. I follow the wire's awkward dance.

"More! Harder, harder!"

My friends follow my orders, keeping their eyes glued to my vibrating silhouette.

"Come on! Jump on the ropes! Hang on them! Take the wood there and bang on them!"

Timid at first, the group gradually throws itself into the game.

"Harder! Harder!" I shriek. "What the hell are you afraid of? Come on! Try to throw me off the wire, damn it!"

Jean-Louis shakes his rope violently, and Mark follows, kicking it with his feet. Soon everyone is jumping up and down, hitting the ropes, screaming and laughing, until I plant one end of the pole in the grass and beg for mercy.

Since I no longer have the use of my legs and arms, I let my body be carried back to the house. The sky has already fallen asleep.

At Annie's suggestion, in the early morning I drive to the village *boulangerie* and bring back a basket brimming with warm croissants. Then I announce my decision to stop filming the coup.

"Either we do a bank robbery, or we do a film about a bank robbery. We cannot do both," I say. "I have decided to do a bank robbery."

Jean-Louis beams.

Yves understands. He picks up the camera and, walking backward with his soundman, films their exit from the house and from the coup.

But where is the cameraman?

Someone screams. It's coming from the big meadow.

Still chewing on croissants, we run outside to find the unfortunate fellow lying on the ground under the Hundred Meters. "I had to give it a try!" he confesses, grinning through his pain.

A couple of hours later, he returns from the Nevers hospital sporting a superb cast and thanks us warmly for our unique hospitality. "Wait!" I say. I go into the house and come back with my New York crutches. "Here, it's a gift, don't lose them!"

I leave everyone else to depart when and how they wish, and Annie to clean and close the old house and hitch a ride back to Paris.

I'm already in my truck, rushing back to Germany. I munch on candy bars and pee in a jar, determined to drive the thousand kilometers nonstop.

"Hi, Francis! Thanks for the money! Bye! See you in New York! Got to go!"

On the way back to Paris, I force the truck to its limit, stopping only for gas.

The phone rings and rings.

"What? Tomorrow morning? You're sure? Oh, that's very nice, thanks!"

It's Jean-Louis, offering to drive Mark and me to the airport. I look at the clock and realize that, thanks to exhaustion, I've just slept twenty hours straight. Nothing is ready. I panic. But I agree to have a long lunch with Paul the Australian, who is just in from London. A thin fellow with short hair, he is as focused and steady as he was during the Sydney walk. He takes his time questioning me.

Patience is rewarded: two hours later, Paul is in.

During the flight, I interrupt Mark from the movie to help stick address labels on a giant stack of my promotional brochures. "After WTC, I'll need those."

Half awake, I ruminate for a rare moment about Annie.

Since long before Vary, she has been angling for an invitation to New York, using tenderness, blackmail, the past, the future, threats, insults, and tears. How disrespectful, how unloving I have been, to evade an answer. But I need absolute detachment, complete freedom. I must be a castaway on the desert island of his dreams, forgotten by all and forced to survive on his wits.

As the plane comes in for a landing, I see through the dirty windows my twin towers, waiting for me.

CUSTOMS

My third arrival in America.

Mark has just passed through customs unchallenged. Why do I always attract suspicion?

"Open up!" orders the towering customs agent.

"What's all this?" he exclaims, eyeing my three battered suitcases brimming with equipment and pointing at the long cylindrical package I can hardly pick up.

Like an amicable salesman, I lift each item slightly in turn, intoning, "Polypropylene ropes, hemp ropes, nylon ropes. Small block-and-tackles with two sheaves, large block-and-tackles with three sheaves. Steel wire-ropes of various diameters. Pulley-blocks for fiber ropes. Safety belts. Construction gloves. Ratchets and monkey wrenches. And, oh, I forgot, a long balancing pole in four sections, complete with assembling inner sleeves!"

"What's all this for?" inquires the frowning giant.

"Oh, nothing. I'm a wirewalker, and I'm here to put a cable between the twin towers of the World Trade Center!"

With a long, loud laugh and gesture toward the exit, the agent replies, "Sure! Welcome and good luck. Next!"

Being of proper upbringing, I smile and murmur, "Thank you."

I HAVE NO IDEA

The next day at lunchtime, Mark and I sneak to the roof of the north tower without a problem.

He takes in the panorama, unconcerned by the void, while I note the changes in the construction site and work on my handstand.

Suddenly, a policeman appears behind us. "Hey, you two, come over here!"

We freeze.

"Do you have any I.D.?"

Eager to prevent Mark from saying anything, I volunteer hurriedly, "No, we don't have any idea! We came here with no idea at all, actually; we just came for the view."

The officer looks at me strangely and turns to Mark: "And you, you have an I.D.?"

Mark opens his mouth, but again I interrupt before he can utter a word. If this cop thinks we have an idea, he must have a suspicion about the reason for our presence. Maybe he has seen me sneaking around here before, maybe he knows everything.

I become agitated, convinced that my answer means life or death for the coup. "No, officer, he does not have any idea either," I say. "He's just a friend, a friend with no idea. Actually, it was my idea to ask him to accompany me to see the view, but you can't really call that an idea. When we're together, it's always me who has ideas. I'm always full of ideas. But today, I assure you, we don't have any ideas, no ideas at all!"

The cop's amusement at my speech and heavy French accent gives way to impatience. He pulls out a notebook and pen. "Come on, guys, I need an I.D., now."

Now that I am silent at last, Mark tactfully explains to me what an I.D. is. We show our passports. The policeman writes down our names and New York address. Like a juggler, he flips shut the pad's heavy cover with a twist of the wrist. With the other hand, he flicks the pen closed in mid-air and returns it to a groove in his leather holster, like John Wayne. "Get out of here! And don't even think of coming back to the roof. I don't ever want to see you guys around these towers again. Is that understood?"

ABORT

Being caught up there—I keep saying "arrested"—slices my dream in two like a saber stroke.

I've crashed back down to earth.

I tell Jim.

I call Jean-Louis, then Annie, then Paul. "*Allo?* We were arrested on the roof. The coup is over!"

To dispel the gloom, I force myself to go hunting for a new site.

I drag myself to Times Square, where I look at tiny reproductions of New York landmarks in the tourist shops and scan all the postcards.

I go sightseeing: the George Washington Bridge, Lincoln Center, Rockefeller Center. I even stare at the tall apartment buildings bordering Central Park.

Nothing.

Nothing can replace the twin towers.

Nothing is dominant enough, proud enough, noble enough.

Discouraged, I dedicate myself to a new season of street-juggling.

It doesn't work. I cannot forget WTC.

Three days after my arrest in the sky, I call Annie: "Please, come over quickly!"

With her by my side, I'll suffer the pain of failure less, I'll feel stronger. Who knows, maybe I'll even succeed in relaunching the coup.

I don't tell anyone, but today I feel life is no longer worth living.

MY FRIEND BARON

The knowledge that Annie is coming fills me with energy.

Mark and I cannot continue to camp out on the floor of Jim's studio. There is barely enough room for his two cats. We go in search of a new home. We answer a couple of classifieds.

I prefer the tiny apartment with only one bedroom and a cramped living room that opens onto a private garden, 12 by 20 feet, where I can practice my juggling. Mark insists on the plush comfort of the old brownstone, very English with its numerous rooms and crystal chandeliers. We introduce ourselves to the tenants, an older couple on their way to Europe. Just as Mark is about to seal the deal, I inquire innocently, "Excuse me, I forgot to mention—I am a juggler and I wanted to know if it was all right with you if I move the Chinese vases to the other room when I practice the large balls in the salon. But don't worry—when I do the flaming torches, of course I'll roll up the antique Persian rug."

Under Mark's black glance, and to my profound astonishment, we're politely escorted to the door.

At the tiny place with the garden at 422 West 22nd Street, we meet Judy, an attractive young actress on her way to Hollywood.

The place is ours if we will agree to take care of the dog for a few days; after that, a neighbor will come to pick it up. On cue, an immense Irish setter bounds from the bedroom (it must have been hiding under the bed), knocks over a chair, and leaps at Mark's neck in a show of passionate affection.

With a smile of revenge, Mark informs our hostess, "Oh, I should tell you, my friend Philippe here really hates an—"

"I really hate an . . . empty apartment," I cut in, not missing a beat. "I love animals! What's his name?"

"Baron."

"Baron? What a beautiful name! Baron, come greet your new friend!" And in front of a flabbergasted Mark, I let my face be licked all over by the drooling giant.

PRELUDE TO AN INTERVIEW

I have decided to attempt to pull off an interview with the workers on the top of the towers, using the flimsy letter of introduction from the architectural digest. I make lists of neutral questions, sensitive questions, information to get, photographs not to miss.

I'll play the journalist, Jim will be my photographer, and Mark the recording engineer. Mark calls the WTC's public relations office. We get an appointment, not for the interview, but first to

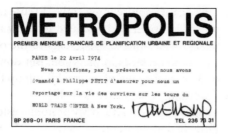

METROPOLIS
PREMIER MENSUEL FRANCAIS DE PLANIFICATION URBAINE ET REGIONALE

PARIS le 22 Avril 1974

Nous certifions, par la présente, que nous avons
demandé à Philippe PETIT d'assurer pour nous un
reportage sur la vie des ouvriers sur les tours du
WORLD TRADE CENTER à New York.

BP 269-01 PARIS FRANCE   TEL 236 79 31

be interviewed ourselves. That's how it works, for security reasons.

Mark and I go to an office on the 68th floor of the north tower. I explain to an affable man with white hair my desire to interview the construction workers toiling on the highest towers in the world, to write an article for a prestigious French architecture magazine.

With a paternalistic smile—the man must already consider us a pair of amateurs—he tells me, "There's no more construction. The towers are built. All the workers are gone, busy now on a new building."

I know he is lying—I've seen plenty of workers during my innumerable clandestine visits—but what can I say? I mention that the magazine had me rent a helicopter recently to take aerial shots, and that during the flight, it seemed to me—yes, I'm quite sure—I saw people working on the unfinished roofs of both towers.

The man is surprised by my insistence. He knows that every journalist wants to ask questions of the renowned "sky-framers" who assemble steel at dizzying heights. "They're famous for their absence of vertigo, you know. And those"—he deliberately slows his delivery, so that this time I may understand—"those, as I told you earlier, have finished their job, they're gone. For two months already. We've got crews of secondary welders, electricians, plasterers, painters, and so on still on the job, mainly on the upper floors of the south tower, but those are not the people you're interested in."

I don't give up so easily.

"On the contrary! I'm tired of all those articles about acrobats taking lunch breaks on narrow I-beams, enough of this high-steel stuff! What I want to write about, what my readers want to know is: Who are those secondary workers no one ever talks about? What are their working conditions? How do they feel? Are they proud? Are they afraid—because they do have vertigo? We need a story on the humble and obscure people putting the finishing touches on the twin towers!"

The man stares at me quite suspiciously. "You said you had a letter of introduction from that magazine? May I see it?"

I hold out the falsified *Metropolis* document, trying to still the trembling of my hand.

The man takes the letter, gives us a long appraisal, reads the letter, pauses, looks me and Mark in the eyes, then orders, "Stay there. I'll be right back."

Mark and I exchange a glance of terror. I turn toward the door. Now's the moment to flee.

But our man soon reappears. "Permission granted. Come back tomorrow."

THE INTERVIEW

The interview goes smoothly.

After talking to a few workers in the upper floors of the south tower, I insist on going to the roof. Our man from the public relations office, trying to be helpful, introduces me to all the contractors and stays close.

By walking around hurriedly, I manage to lose him whenever I need to give discreet directions to Jim or Mark.

"Jim, right there!" I whisper, brushing by him, directing three fingers glued together (so it doesn't look like I am pointing) to an I-beam that interests me.

Jim focuses his camera on a group of workers spreading

cement, but at the instant of clicking the shutter, he turns the camera covertly to the I-beam in question.

"Mark, he's all yours for two minutes!" I murmur, retying my shoelaces.

Mark sticks the too-large microphone of his toylike tape recorder—bought yesterday at Woolworth—under the nose of our host and asks, in a reporter's obnoxious I-have-a-right-to-know tone, for some clarifications on trivial points. The man frowns at the instrument, probably thinking, "These French journalists are so cheap," but he responds with lengthy explanations, during which I speed unimpeded to an area I need to inspect.

When the spokesman is not too close, I start bits of conversation with the workers. Under cover of my less-than-fluent English, I succeed in gleaning information about their work schedules, locker room locations, entry routes, security conditions, and countless other details relevant to the coup. I also learn the correct terms for the different features of the roof.

Our guide is obviously intrigued by the constant dispersal and regrouping of this weird trio of journalists and their unusual style of questioning. Naturally, he focuses on me. He seems impressed by my perfect knowledge of the towers, but he's a bit mystified.

I'm pleased at his consternation when I address several workers in their native tongues, conversing in turn in French, Russian, German, and Spanish.

But when I ask a passing architect if I can take a look at his blueprints, and inquire whether he knows why the towers are not true twins, why they're of different heights, the PR man orders, "Stop the tape recorder! Who gave you that information? No one knows that besides a couple of engineers."

Keeping my cool, I crouch and point at the other roof, squinting. "Well, it's obvious! No?"

The spokesman, in a sweat, crouches and squints his eyes. Now he is confused! Mark and Jim turn quickly to conceal their silent laughter.

Back on the ground, Jim rushes his film to the lab, Mark busies himself transcribing his tapes, and I, all smiles, put my notes and sketches in order.

The success of this first "official" intrusion seems to bring the coup closer to . . .

To reality?

INSIDE MY VEINS

I am encouraged.

Encouraged enough to resume looking for the equipment still lacking.

Not far from the island of Manhattan, I discover a cable factory, or rather a cable factory's warehouse and workshop.

Finding myself surrounded by hundreds of coils of steel wire-rope of different constructions and diameters; lifting enormous U- or Lyra-shackles one after another off the greasy concrete floor; caressing the grain left by the foundry on heavy-duty thimbles; comparing the design of cable clamps that jingle when I pick them up and put them back; and chatting under dim lights with men who have dedicated their lives to handling the unforgiving steel, who have black grease forever imprinted on their skin—and who love it—all this rekindles from embers to living flames my determination to fight for my mad project.

Thus, like the pair of impassable towering shadows that peacefully stretch every evening above the rooftops of the voracious metropolis as if to invade it, as if to force it to surrender, as if to suffocate it; like these two silvery pylons whose summits deface the clouds, and between which the sun must sneak in order to chase out the last of the night; similarly, inexorably, my insane dream of the twin towers has once again infiltrated my veins, has once again become essential to my existence.

Silent emptiness prolongs this thought.

DEAR JEAN-LOUIS ...

Dear Jean-Louis:

The coup is back on!

We have a new home. The interview was a success. I got all the information and all the photographs I was missing. I found out why we were arrested—we weren't wearing helmets. I found all the equipment (except the Tirfor). Paul the Australian is arriving tomorrow, Annie is joining me soon ...

Now you can come to New York.

Let's do it!

Philippe

Jean-Louis receives the letter exactly ten days after the arrest. He reads between the lines that I could not have reorganized anything so quickly, especially considering that I spent most of that time regaining my lost enthusiasm. But he thinks if he comes he'll be able to impose a serious plan and push the coup to victory. If he waits for impeccable organization, he'll never see New York!

He asks for two weeks' leave and his boss replies, "No way! One week, and not an hour more!"

ULTIMATUM

When Jean-Louis lands, I'm at JFK to greet him.

It's May 25; the coup is set for the twenty-seventh.

No. Having barely said hello to Mark and Paul, we argue all afternoon, then change it to the thirtieth.

My friend accuses me. He says my "colossal preparations" are impractical and unintelligent.

I'm discouraged and furious.

He's furious and discouraged, to see the coup so close to success and yet so sure to fail. He can tell I haven't figured out how to enter the towers and get to a hiding place, that I don't have all the equipment. He's convinced there's not enough time.

"Why can't you stop kidding yourself and face reality!" he reproaches.

I spend the evening defending myself from his accusations.

We fall asleep arguing.

In the morning, we pretend to forget our differences.

I pull out the yellow pages and ask Mark and Paul to round up a Tirfor, the crucial cable-tensioning device, also known as a T-35 or a come-along, which does not wrap the cable onto a winch but passes it through the machine, as if inside two giant hands were pulling. Paul remembers that we used one for the illegal walk in Sydney, but here no one seems to know what we're talking about.

Meanwhile, Jean-Louis and I, smelling equipment in the air, argue over rigging details. Soon Mark and Paul try to assert their own vision of the coup, but I no longer translate. Gradually, two groups form and confront each other: the French against the Australians.

Evening, then night, fail to diffuse the quarrel between Jean-Louis and me, and the tired Australians end up falling asleep in front of the TV.

It's 5 a.m.

"Jean-Louis, I don't understand . . . You're trying again to change what we agreed on in Vary!"

"It's not that you don't understand! It's that you don't want to understand! So here it is. You do it my way, or I stop right here!"

I think of the coup. I exhale, "Good-night-Jean-Louis."

"Where do you guys come from? C'mon, tell me, don't be shy!"

I hate these tourist-trap electronics stores in the vicinity of Times Square, where an overzealous salesman must become your best friend before he rips you off. But they've got a big selection, and you can open the boxes.

The solid, bearded young sales clerk follows us through the shop, repeating in his crass American accent, "Can I help you with something?"

"Yeah, leave us alone," I say in French to Jean-Louis, as we lean over a glass counter to examine the walkie-talkies and intercoms.

"Ah! Communications! You came to the right place!" loudly exclaims our persistent friend, clapping his hands proudly. "I've got exactly what you need!"

I growl to Jean-Louis in French, "This guy is starting to get on my nerves!"

We return to comparing intercoms, but the salesman cuts in again. "You don't want an antiquated intercom; you want the best walkie-talkie in town—here!" In my limited, heavily accented English, I ask firmly to be left alone.

"Sure, man! Don't get upset! Call me when you need me, I'll be right here!" He moves twelve inches down the counter and buries his face in a thick radio catalog.

Finally feeling free to talk, Jean-Louis and I converse in rapid French, reviewing our options. A walkie-talkie or any other cordless device is definitely out because of the police and radio hackers. What we need is a lightweight, long-range intercom with a 200-foot cord and an adjustable ring in case a guard shows up. We discuss the difficulties of stringing the cord across in the dark. It's hard for us to choose, but I discourage Jean-Louis from asking the salesman for help, adding in loud French, "Don't you see he's the American cliché? He doesn't know anything, doesn't give a damn; all he wants is to get rid of his stuff at the highest price."

Almost in answer, the young man leans over and starts pouring advice over us. But underneath his crudeness—which must come with the job—our salesman actually reminds me of Jean-Louis: he is down-to-earth, confident, persuasive, and smart, and he has the same sly grin at the corner of his mouth. He knows what he is talking about, and in no time, we buy the right items.

As he escorts us to the door, the salesman whispers in perfect French, using Parisian slang: "I couldn't help overhearing what you guys were talking about. If it's a bank robbery you're working on, you better be more discreet; there're a lot of us Frenchmen here in Manhattan!" And in an even lower voice, he adds, "It's okay with me, I've got nothing against bank robbers!"

Stunned, Jean-Louis and I exchange a grin.

"We invite him to dinner, Philippe?"

"We invite him to dinner, Jean-Louis?"

By evening, good old Jean-Pierre—a certified expat Parisian, who insists upon being called JP—has joined the WTC Association and is congratulating himself on having accepted our invitation to break bread.

"Yes," I say, "you came to the right place!"

"When do I start?" our new friend asks.

"Now," I reply. "Go call the store and leave a message: you're sick. You and I are driving to Boston tomorrow to get a cable-puller."

COME ALONG

JP and I drive to Boston, stopping only for gas and to call the warehouse manager—the man we've befriended by phone during our many morning calls from New York—to announce our imminent arrival and to ensure that he stays open for us.

The drive is longer than we thought, and the directions more complex.

We call again. By the time we reach Boston, which we have crossed twice by mistake, it is half an hour past the warehouse's closing time and we still have not located our destination on the map. One last call puts us back on track and assures us the man is still waiting.

The sun is low when JP parks the car near a row of loading docks. All the metal shutters are down. Above the factory, a few windows are lit, but the warehouse is closed. In front of the warehouse stands a man in blue overalls, a wooden crate at his feet.

JP makes the introductions. I rip open the crate.

I make sure the machine is a come-along—a Tirfor, or Griphoist as it is called in America. After trying for weeks to locate one, I've become an expert on the subject. I check its 3.5-ton pulling capacity, the extra security pins hidden inside the handle, and the fire-tapered tip of the specially manufactured cable that comes with it.

Then I thank the man profusely and load the machine into the backseat of the car while JP slips him a few bucks.

"Fabulous! A free Tirfor!" I exclaim. But JP persuades me to stop at the office. The door is open, the receptionist and secretaries long gone. There is light upstairs; I hear a voice. We climb. A door labeled PRESIDENT is ajar, and we enter.

"I'll call you back," says the president, startled as he turns his expensive leather desk chair toward the intruders. "Who the hell are you? How did you get in?"

"Philippe Petit. By the door."

"What do you want?"

"To buy a Griphoist, a T-35."

"The factory is closed!"

"But we've come all the way from New York City . . . "

"What company are you?"

"I'm me! I'm no company!"

"We don't sell retail. You need to go through a dealer."

"But listen, I am a high wire artist! I have a very, very big show soon! And I absolutely need . . . Look!" Beneath the eyes of the important man, I flip through the photographs and clippings in the thick album with which I always travel.

The man looks at the book, at my face, and gradually his aggression lessens as he grows intrigued. "What makes you think I can provide a T-35 just like that, huh? I usually need a week's warning. I'm not even sure we have any in the warehouse."

"Well, I'm sure!" I say.

The president laughs. "Oh, you're in charge! I thought I was running things here."

"I'm sure . . . because I just loaded one in our car!" I confess, trying hard not to look triumphant.

"What?!" exclaims our host, annoyance once again invading his features.

JP jumps in and explains our ordeal in locating the machine, our endless telephone conversations, our long drive, our rush to arrive on time. He manages to omit any mention of why and how the machine ended up inside our car.

By now, I'm ready for the kill. Before the president can come to his senses, I start doing magic tricks as a preamble to the deal I have in mind. Flipping more pictures from the album for my captive audience, I propose, "Give us the come-along for free, and I'll invite you to the giant event I'm preparing!"

The president declines, but to JP's astonishment, he agrees to sell us the machine at cost and wishes us the best.

The sky is getting dark as JP points the speeding car vigilantly toward Manhattan, while I, leaning back over the front seat, keep caressing the rough metal casing of my new come-along, asleep in the rear.

STREET MAINTENANCE

250 feet of galvanized steel wire-rope, ⅞ inch in diameter, 6 x 19 construction (made up of 6 strands, each containing 19 wires), is definitely too heavy for one person to carry.

Jean-Louis rolls the coil of cable down the stairs to the street and proceeds to lay it out at full length on the asphalt, not straight down the middle of the road, but not too close to the parked cars, either, in order to clean it as instructed.

He holds the coil vertically between his knees, using one hand to untie each of the numerous bits of twine securing the package, and the other to gently pay out the greasy, cumbersome cable, a loop at a time. I've warned him that if he lets go of the coil, the wire will spring out in all directions, injuring him and making a giant mess that will take hours to untangle.

On the sidewalk, passersby are intrigued.

Jean-Louis leaves the cable laid from one end of the block to the other and goes to fetch a bucket of gasoline, a bag of rags, and a handful of white towels. Oblivious to the small crowd of neighbors who have gathered, he gets down on his knees and proceeds to clean the cable. Vehicles slow down to avoid hitting him. Someone calls the police.

A patrol car drives up the block very slowly, creeping alongside the entire length of the cable, and stops near the end, where Jean-Louis is on his knees.

The window rolls down. The two cops watch.

Jean-Louis keeps working.

One of the officers, a very big man, gets out of the car, adjusting his cap. "Hey, you! What the hell is going on here?"

Without pausing in his work, Jean-Louis replies in his broken, heavily accented English, "Oh, nossing! Me . . . friend wirewalker, he . . . big show tomorrow, me . . . clean cable!"

"Uh-huh. Well, guess what?" snarls the cop. "Me . . . police. Me . . . come back half hour. You . . . still here, you . . . big trouble! Got that?"

Still focusing on his task, Jean-Louis silently nods.

The door slams. The police leave. The neighbors go home.

Night has fallen when, by luck, JP finds a parking place just in front of 422 West 22nd Street and wakes me up with a sonorous "We're back!"

I cannot believe my sleepy eyes: Jean-Louis is on the front stoop, trying to roll the enormous coil of the cable up the stairs all by himself.

An expert glance informs me the cable has been magnificently cleaned.

I ask Jean-Louis why Mark and Paul are not helping.

"The Australians?" answers my friend with disgust. "You have no idea! We spent the day bickering." And he explains how, after I left with JP for Boston, they refused to do anything, insisting they could do nothing without my approval. They barely agreed to keep an eye on the cable drying in the street while Jean-Louis took over their job, that of getting the missing tools.

"Imagine me, looking all over the city for stores that sell tools, not even knowing how it's called in English! Now I know, it's called '*arrd-wear-storr*'!" By then it was closing time, and when Jean-Louis got back to the house exhausted and found Paul and Mark on the steps trading jokes, he got mad. "I told them we had to get together and prepare as much of the stuff as possible so that we could do the coup tomorrow. I told them I could not stay an extra day. I said—all this in my bad English, imagine!—I said if the coup does not happen tomorrow, it will not happen at all. And you know what this twisted Paul comes up with? He tells me that you and he have to have a talk, that your security is at stake, he's not willing to encourage a suicide, things like that. While I'm killing myself to finish cleaning the cable and roll it, all alone! They really have no guts, those two! Go talk to them. Maybe you can squeeze a little something out of them. But to me it's hopeless."

I go talk.

Hiding my fury and lying through my teeth, I assure my Australian friends that I will be the first one to give up, if and when my safety or their security is at stake. I explain it's not too late to unite our efforts; we can work part of the night and be ready for JP when he brings the truck at eleven in the morning. I guarantee there's not much to it after that, just to hurry to the roof, maybe hiding a while and helping to pass the cable across.

Despair is a fine acting coach: Mark and Paul believe me. For a few hours they are back to work. But as the night stretches on, their confidence thins. By 2 a.m., they are demanding a forum.

"Give up!" I say, having no taste for talking to them.

The Australians give up. They abandon the coup. They go to sleep.

Feverishly, Jean-Louis assists me in rolling, tying, making packages. Our plan is to work all night, finish in time for the 11 a.m. delivery, and hope that, after eight hours of sleep, our rested Australians will see that everything is ready and not have the heart to refuse to join us.

Dawn is spying on us from behind the window. The race against time seems futile.

A fever takes over my being; an extreme fatigue grounds me and grinds me into bits of intense despair. I have reached a point of no return on the road to disbelief. I am sure we won't be ready on time. We haven't even decided, Jean-Louis and I, the latest directives, once in the towers, once on the roof. The plan twirls and whirls inside my skull until the evidence escapes in drilling pain, as if during a trepanation: "We don't have a plan! "Bereft of all faith, yet awaiting a miracle, I continue to gather equipment and to pack, like some beheaded animal. All the while I focus an energy I no longer possess on keeping my eyelids open. I do not understand why my body does not fall asleep on the floor.

We are one cardboard box short.

Mechanically, Jean-Louis goes out into the early morning streets and comes back brandishing two large empty boxes— "for you to choose"—still dripping with dead fish and broken eggs. He simply emptied the garbage they contained onto the sidewalk.

We laugh at our madness.

I fill one stinking box to the rim as Jean-Louis catches his breath. But when we try to pick it up, the bottom gives out, spilling the contents all over the carpet. All of our boxes are much too heavy to move, and much too weak for their loads. And it is 7 a.m.

We should start all over again. This is dementia.

Jean-Louis asks me what I think of the situation. In answer, I go into the bedroom and close the door. I collapse on the mattress, unable to keep tears of rage and exhaustion from burning my cheeks. But minutes later, I compose myself and calmly join Jean-Louis for an early morning chat—about life, death, and the universe—until we decide it's not too early to tell JP the coup is a complete failure.

Is there another kind?

FORTUNE COOKIES

Seeing how devastated I am, Jean-Louis attempts to rebuild hope. He advises me to call everyone with the news that the coup has been postponed, instead of saying that it failed. He suggests I not throw the Australians out on the street yet. He promises to try to take a new leave of absence from his job in a few months, when I will have had a chance to reorganize the coup. He offers to accompany me to the airport to welcome Annie. He proposes that the three of us have dinner in Chinatown tonight . . .

It's still morning, and I have an idea.

I wake Paul gently and ask him for a last favor: to call WTC and request a visit to the roof. He has bragged about a letter he's obtained from an eminent architect in London, recommending that Paul be allowed to visit and photograph the top of WTC to complete his survey of high structures. I have the telephone number for a department other than public relations.

Happy to feel needed and to diffuse yesterday's sourness, Paul calls immediately. When he hangs up, he announces that he has permission to conduct the survey this afternoon, and to bring a photographer.

Am I up to that? I know nothing about photography. What about picking up Annie?

Jean-Louis encourages me to go as the photographer. I'll be able to survey the roof in peace, I'll be able to take shots of what interests me—an extraordinary opportunity! He figures out everything, down to the bus schedule: he'll even lend me his expensive cameras. We'll ride together to the airport, and on the bus he'll give me a crash course in photography; he'll wait and pick up Annie while I ride back to Manhattan, arriving just in time for the survey appointment. "If we go now, you can make it!"

Despite mental distress and physical exhaustion, I attend carefully to Jean-Louis's crash course, and by the end of an hour-and-a-half bus ride, I am a photographer.

"What a fine day," says the architectural consultant as he gives Paul and me a tour of the deserted roof of the north tower. Indeed, the sun is warming the air, there is no wind, and even I calm down and enjoy the view.

Understanding that we have an agenda, our considerate guide offers to leave us alone for a while. He has some stationery with him and wishes to sit by the crane and write a letter while he works on his tan.

Freely and peacefully for the first time, I scout the roof. Paul walks around, keeping an eye on our guide.

I direct my cameras wherever I wish and take a number of priceless shots. I can inspect the locations where I'm considering anchoring the cable, comparing, studying, kneeling to appreciate a detail. It's paradise!

I'm about to arrive at a solution when Paul interrupts; he

judges we've been glued too long to the corner facing the south tower. "We've got to move! He's going to suspect something!"

Can't he see the consultant is absorbed in his letter?

To get rid of Paul and to create a diversion, I send him circling the roof.

He returns a moment later and tells me he wants us to leave.

A violent, albeit hushed fight follows.

My anger does not dissipate Paul's growing anxiety. It's his time on the tower, it's his appointment, he says, and he decrees that we must go immediately. On the verge of panic, he breaks away and pulls the official from his writing, to tell him that we're finished with our survey.

Backing up toward the stairs—I want to snap one last picture—I trip and fall into a nest of steel beams, smacking both of Jean-Louis's cameras.

Back home, beat with fatigue and disgust, I kick the door open with my boot and throw myself into Annie's arms for a second, before pulling her into the bedroom and slamming the door.

Instead of asking about her flight, I pour on her all my rage and misery: I've been fighting nonstop with Jean-Louis, the Australians have given up, Paul is completely mad, I may have wrecked Jean-Louis's cameras. "And with all this, I couldn't even be at the airport for you!"

Annie braces me, and I go talk to Jean-Louis about his cameras. Although they are still operative, they will need repair. But when I offer to street-juggle to pay for it, Jean-Louis tells me not to worry, it's part of doing the coup.

Then I return to Annie and resume my bitter narration of the past few weeks, concluding, torn and eviscerated, "You see, I can't count on anybody! The coup is impossible anyway!"

"So give up!" answers Annie, to my astonishment. "Until now, you've always attacked mountains, and you've always triumphed. But there are mountains that can't be conquered. Give up! You

83

were on the way to killing yourself. Or else by some miracle you'd do the walk and be a dot in the sky. No one would even see you—it would be almost ugly. Give up! Think of all the things you want to do. You could go back to Vary, put a high wire act together, be hired by Circus Sarrasani, and share the bill with Francis Brunn. You have so many dreams!"

Jean-Louis succeeds in pulling us out of the house. We leave the Australians to their sulking guilt and run to Chinatown. Without asking my opinion, Jean-Louis buys three tickets for a Bruce Lee movie (knowing he's my favorite). After dinner, he breaks the fortune cookies, passing the slips of paper to Annie to read and rolling them into spitballs to shoot at me with his straw.

I try to smile and laugh with my friends.

I can't.

From left to right: Jean-Louis, Mark, Paul, Philippe and Jim

At 6 p.m. the next evening, Annie and Jean-Louis, obviously exhausted, stagger through the door and collapse on the sofa, laughing. They throw their shoes across the living room and stare at the ceiling for a second, then turn to me and exclaim at the same time, "Philippe, you're not going to believe it! But it's true, and we have the pictures to prove it!"

In the morning, with hope and hopelessness still colliding in the air like drunken birds, I'd had nothing better to share with Jean-Louis than bitter regret: "It's a shame you're going back to Paris without even seeing what my towers look like!"

Answering his own curiosity and probably wanting to boost my morale, my friend decided to give it a try, and to bring his cameras "just in case." I encouraged Annie to go as well: "You really should see how beautiful it is up there. Plus, a nice couple is the ideal guise to deflect suspicion." It was my turn to give Jean-Louis a crash course: on how to sneak to the top. And off they went.

I stayed all day in front of the too-loud television to keep my brain from attempting to analyze my fresh disaster, and so I would not have to deal with the Australians, who glided by like ghosts.

Now I'm dying to know the result of Annie and Jean-Louis's expedition.

Not sparing any details, they proudly retrace their race to the top of the south tower. They describe getting lost, being sent back down, trying all the elevators; they even mime their *moment de bravoure* eluding a guard in the stairs. On the roof, Jean-Louis became exuberant. Forgetting his fear of the void, he went close to the edge and took some pictures. On his way down, all the way on his way down, he emphasizes, he kept taking pictures—pictures of each door Annie held open for him, each stairwell, each corridor, each dead end—until they found themselves safe and sound on the carpet of the mezzanine.

"I'll process them myself. You'll see!" promises Jean-Louis. "And you're quite right, it's fabulous up there!"

For the first time, my friend talks about the coup with zeal. For the first time, we discuss the past organization without rancor. For the first time, we joyfully build plans for the future. Jean-Louis turns his back to the Australians watching TV and concludes, "With a couple of really good guys, there's no way we can fail!"

I am already on the phone inviting Jim Moore to join our trio for a "last supper" in Chinatown. And this time it's I who shoot spitballs at Jean-Louis, as Annie and Jim try to keep score.

The next morning, Jean-Louis is gone.

The Australians leave soon thereafter. I find Paul's farewell gift on the coffee table: sketches of possible cavaletti configurations. I must confess, some of his concepts are brilliant.

I am left alone, with a taste of defeat on my tongue. I need to rest. I need to think. I need to bail out the sinking ship of my mind.

"You're not alone," says Annie, who refuses to talk about WTC, advocates giving up, and will only visit the city she finds so dirty and dangerous if I'll come with her. Back in Paris she heard so many stories about New York's stray bullets and muggings, she won't even go by herself to the grocery store on Ninth Avenue.

Fine. I sleep two days straight. When I wake up, Annie is in the garden. Waiting for me to take her out, she has taken up a new pastime—feeding the neighborhood cats. And these bold felines already have the nerve to consider the apartment their new home.

Great.

Let's go visit New York.

WTC EVERYWHERE

It starts with Chinatown.

After three hours of inundation by colors, smells, and noises, Annie pulls me aside for respite at a little stone arch with benches, next to a phone booth that looks like a pagoda. Suddenly I spring up. "My god! This is one of the best places in Manhattan to view them, look!" I exclaim, pointing excitedly at the twin towers.

Next, the arts.

We hop from gallery to gallery in SoHo, do MoMA until the closing bell rings. But here, there, everywhere, I am oblivious to the treasures I run past. I am brought to a stop only by an image of the city's skyline, unmistakably featuring the World Trade Center. "Hey . . . that's a neat piece!"

We wait on line with the tourists—argh, I hate that!—to reach the observation deck atop the Empire State Building, where Annie allows the telescope to steal all my change. The first thing, the only thing I look at when it's my turn, is of course— "Annie! Incredible! My towers . . . You can see every detail of the roof with this! Wouldn't it be incredible to find myself up there one day? Wouldn't it be magnificent?"

Annie, sheltering her eyes from the sun, is not looking at WTC. She's examining my face, wondering if I can survive without attacking those giants.

The nightmare that wakes me the next morning gives her the answer.

I sit up suddenly, covered in sweat, and rip the sheets from

87

my body. I have been screaming my despair in my sleep.

"Listen," Annie whispers, caressing my face. "Since it's impossible for you to forget the coup, then go for it! But remember, all the preparations you've done so far have been of no use. So go back. Start fresh, redo everything. I'll go with you, I'll help you!"

"NEW ORGANISATION"

The garden is full of birds conversing through the thick foliage, the street full of kids screaming at play until dinnertime. The city is singing its early-summer song.

I grab my new sketchpad: 9 by 12 inches, fifty sheets of extra-heavy paper, glued and bound. FOR PASTELS WATER COLORS CRAYONS PENCILS INKS, reads the cover. AND HIGH WIRE, I add.

You open, you see: twin towers drawn with one continuous line; a wire on top; on the wire, a little five-pointed star—you know, the kind you doodle quickly, without lifting the pen. And under the drawing, in caps, "WTC" with a subtitle in lowercase: "new organisation"—French spelling, you have a problem with that?

LOST & FOUND PART I

How to start anew?

By getting what's missing.

I become a habitué of Canal Street, the mecca of hardware stores, where I rummage incessantly for tools and equipment. I visit warehouses in the different boroughs. I crisscross Manhattan, now teeming with tourists unfazed by the unbearable heat and the piles of garbage obstructing the sidewalks.

Annie follows me everywhere.

"We're losing time!" I complain each time the laces of her sandals break, forcing me to look in the garbage for something to repair them.

Today, to celebrate the "new organisation," I escape, alone, open to influence. I've decided to drift freely through the city.

And I find myself . . . guess where?

I'm strolling through the lobby of the towers, daydreamingly indifferent to the lunchtime rush, when someone calls my name.

A tall man in a three-piece suit walks toward me. He is young and slender, with long black hair and an outrageous handlebar moustache above a long, narrow beard. Something about this intelligent-looking man strikes me as challenging, as mysterious. His voice, as I expected—isn't that odd?—is calm and sober, with a je ne sais quoi . . . He says he saw me street-juggling in Paris last year. The sound of my voice surprises him; inside my circle of chalk, I never say a word. He congratulates me on my performance, which he describes eloquently, then inquires, with a cryptic smile, "But what are you doing in this neck of the woods? You don't belong to the world of trade. This isn't the sort of place one would expect to make your acquaintance."

I return his question.

He explains that he works in the buildings.

"Which building?"

"The south tower."

"Which floor?"

"Eighty-second floor."

Only 28 floors below the roof!

He introduces himself. We exchange a firm handshake. He goes back to the group of businessmen he was with and disappears, absorbed by the crowd.

Fantastic!

I am going to befriend this strange fellow who works on the 82nd floor and knows me. I am going to make him an accomplice.

Almost dancing with delight, I run home, impatient to announce the miracle to Annie. But on the way, I freeze: I have forgotten his name. I have forgotten which tower! I did not ask for his phone number.

I share with Annie victory and defeat.

What to do?

I can't go to the 82nd floor of each tower, questioning people and staring at every employee's face.

For three days, I hide inside a telephone booth at lunchtime, watching intently the comings-and-goings of hundreds, thousands of hungry employees in search of a snack.

No black-bearded giant.

PUBLIC RELATIONS

Whenever hopelessness sets in, the antidote is street-juggling.

I'm making quite a scene every afternoon on the tiny sidewalk of Grand Army Plaza, near the circular steps of the lovely white fountain overlooked by the ritzy Plaza Hotel.

I usually get a crowd of two or three hundred. People stand four rows deep into the street, people climb on the hoods of parked cars. The police are restless to catch me; I escape them with my unicycle.

People bring their friends. The word gets around. The press hears.

Today, June 24, 1974, there's a nice interview on page 57 of the *Daily News* by the columnist Sidney Fields. And a nice picture of my face, too.

I give details of the preparations I made for my illegal wire walks in Paris and Sydney. I'm quoted as planning one for New York City, "between the roofs of the world." I refuse to give the location, call it "a big surprise." I do give the times and places of my upcoming street performances.

The next day, a professional mike and a television camera with its little red light on show up in the front row.

Not saying a word, I invite the woman holding the mike into the circle. She's desperate to have me talk. Instead, I mime playfully around her before I return her to her place, presenting her with a departure gift—her watch! When the applause calms down, she turns to the camera: "This is Melba Tolliver for Channel 7 Eyewitness News, live in front of Grand Army Plaza: I did not get my interview, but I got my watch back!" Waving the *Daily News*, she concludes by mentioning my upcoming illegal high wire walk—"but when and where . . . Nobody knows!"

Later, in a dark office, several employees take their eyes away from a wall of electronic screens under their surveillance and break into a noisy exchange. One of them holds up an article from the *Daily News* for his coworkers to read. Another says he saw the same guy on TV, stealing a watch. The newspaper clipping is pinned to the bulletin board. "Okay fellas, this one is for us. He's gonna put his wire here soon. We better watch out."

They are still laughing when someone passes his head through the door. "Hey guys, got a minute? Come see what I found in the stairs on the seventy-fourth floor, some kind of weird fresco . . . "

Everyone leaves. The door slams shut, rattling the pane of glass that reads:

WORLD TRADE CENTER

SECURITY HEADQUARTERS

"So you're happy now? You got what you wanted?" Annie reproaches me after reading the article and watching the news.

True, I might be recognized, I might have to work ten times more cautiously, a hundred times harder. But now that I have announced the coup to millions of New Yorkers, there is absolutely no way I can give up!

More impetuous than ever, I keep planning, religiously logging my progress in the "New Organisation" *cahier*. I keep hunting for the mysterious man with the handlebar moustache, showing up at lunchtime in the lobbies, incognito under a Tyrolean hat and large sunglasses.

Got him!

I literally run to him and block his path.

He repeats his surprise at seeing me here, and again observes I do not belong in such a crowd . . . Why the persistent smile?

His name is Barry Greenhouse, he works on the 82nd floor of the south tower, his direct number is . . .

Annie and I take him to dinner, along with my thick photo album.

Before the appetizers, Barry has seen everything of my performing past.

Why is he grinning so much? Does he guess?

In the middle of the main course, I start blabbing about my love for the city, about its skyline. Barry leans back, like a cigar aficionado before exhaling smoke. He smiles intently and stares calmly at me, waiting for me to tell him what he already knows.

I throw onto his plate the entire coup, raw.

He asks two or three pertinent questions and, satisfied with my answers, gently, almost elegantly, whispers, "I'm in."

I order three desserts, all for me.

LOOKING FOR DIRECTION

Here and there, up and down, left and right—meandering the path of my dreams, I often wake up lost.

Not tonight.

It's 3 a.m. and it has been decided. In my sleep.

I will start walking from the south tower.

And if I walk more than once, I will conclude the performance at the south tower.

Why?

Some will see in my choice the ocean breathing encouragingly behind me at the time of the first step, and, in front, my eyes set upon a multitude of roofs, of homes sheltering the inhabitants, my audience.

Some may remember that the south tower was the first with which I came into contact, with my chin, long ago. The tower I never visited at first, the mysterious one.

And some, more pragmatic, might say, "It's because of that damned wind, always blowing from the Verrazano Bridge . . ."

I shrug to Annie, "I know it's 2 a.m.! But I must return it in the morning, I rented it."

Yesterday, I spotted a piano and refrigerators being moved into the neighborhood. Otherwise I never would have had the idea of using a mover's intricate hand dolly to bring the equipment up the stairs of WTC on the day of the coup.

It was hard to locate one; they're rare here. In France, it's a common piece of equipment called *le diable*, the devil—don't ask me why.

It has two long, curved handles, like a wheelbarrow's, at the top, and at the bottom, on each side, three wheels linked by a rubber caterpillar belt. It is specially designed to bring heavy loads up and down stairs.

I stack as many bricks stolen from a nearby construction site as *le diable* will carry on his shoulders. Furtively, I open the door and sneak onto the carpeted staircase of my sleeping four-story building. I don't mean anyone any harm; I only want to practice.

I start my ascent quietly, but the machine squeaks under the load, bangs into the railing, and gets stuck every two steps. Plus a bunch of daring bricks try to make it back to the construction site. A particularly bold one manages to run down an entire flight of stairs before I catch her.

Left and right, apartments are waking up.

I take a break on the third floor. I unload *le diable* one brick at a time, quietly, determined to find out what's wrong with the caterpillar. I stack the bricks on one of the thick doormats, without a sound.

That's when old Mrs. Janets in 3-A—her white hair full of pink plastic rollers—opens her door. She looks at the 3-foot-high brick structure a mad, barefoot mason is building in the middle of the night to wall her in. Before slamming her door in terror, she manages to utter, "What the devil . . . ?"

She's right.

I keep trying to improve the system, climbing up and down the stairs as discreetly as I can, while worried neighbors spy on me from behind chained doors. At last the Luddite in me decides to bring the impractical machine back to the apartment. I fall asleep with the satisfying fantasy of my crew hoisting nearly a ton of equipment up the towers on our shoulders, like the builders of the pyramids.

Historians, take note: I did bring back the hundred bricks to my fellow masons the following night, but could not resist arranging them on the ground into a pretty question mark.

NEW ACCESSORIES

What better way to find out how heavy equipment enters the towers than to organize a phony delivery?

Barry agrees to receive the goods.

But first I need two new accomplices to replace the Australians.

I learn that Jim Moore is struggling to remove the linoleum flooring of his newly acquired loft at the corner of Hudson and Chambers. We spend two days breaking our nails and dulling blades: the linoleum is glued to the wood with some kind of tar and breaks off only an inch at a time. Each time we take a rest, I discuss WTC. Again I ask my friend to help on the roof. Again the answer is no.

The next morning, two Americans who live in the building bump into Jim in the lobby and ask if his friend the Frenchman—they've passed me in the elevator—is the tightrope walker, the guy who's looking for a place to put his wire. They recognized me from the article and the TV.

"Uh-huh," mumbles Jim.

"Well, you can tell him we've come up with a terrific idea, a site that will blow his mind."

"What's that?"

"The top of the World Trade Center!"

Well trained, Jim breaks out laughing, but thinks to ask—in case his friend Philippe loves the idea—would they be ready to help him?

Receiving an enthusiastic chorus in response, Jim arranges a meeting.

Annie and I show up the next day, upstairs in a dark loft.

Donald, with curved shoulders and long, thinning hair in a ponytail, is at the piano whining out a new song in a high-pitched voice; he's a rock musician. Chester, with thick glasses and a bushy head of hair atop a body too long and too thin, pouts sadly. He is a carpenter.

I show the album, I open the *cahiers*, I display accordions of WTC pictures. Donald and Chester are astounded by the extent of my preparations. They are ready to take part. I ask them to promise not to tell anyone, and they do.

I don't suffer dismal faces gladly, and I don't appreciate rock and roll music, but I have no choice.

ARCHITECTURAL BEQUEST

Without telling me, just prior to his disappearance Paul had written a letter to Emery Roth and Sons, the firm that designed the towers, introducing himself as an architecture scholar and requesting help in his study of WTC.

The protective envelope I tear open this morning spills out its priceless contents all over the sofa: ten off-white sheets, 18 by 25 inches, covered with blueprints:

1ST FLOOR
9TH TO 16TH FLOOR
35TH TO 40TH FLOOR
44TH FLOOR / SKY LOBBY
50TH TO 54TH FLOOR
78TH FLOOR / SKY LOBBY
96TH TO 100TH FLOOR
107TH FLOOR / RESTAURANT LEVEL

There is also a superb 9TH TO 10TH FLOOR/CORE PLAN, plus a gorgeous CROSS SECTION THRU TYPICAL FLOOR detailing men's and women's toilets and clearly showing the suspended ceiling and the lost space above it, which I've already explored and deemed an excellent hiding place. I measured its height to be 3'6". Here, the drawing indicates 4'0" from suspended ceiling to the top of the 4-inch concrete slab; that's a height of 3'8". Well, nobody's perfect. I earmark the sheet, though; after the coup I'll check, maybe it's *their* mistake . . .

A kid on Christmas Day, I rummage through my WTC files and compare the few old and out-of-sequence blueprints (which "fell into my bag" during my countless shadow visits) with the pristine documents destiny has just awarded me.

Although instantly my most prized possession, this bunch of blueprints is perfectly useless. Nonetheless, they make me feel professional: when you plan a bank robbery, first you acquire blueprints, right?

"Hey, you!"

One of Annie's feral kittens is walking on the 78th floor— peeing on the elevator shaft! I grab the trespasser by the tail and send it flying into the garden. The cliché is true: they do always land on their feet.

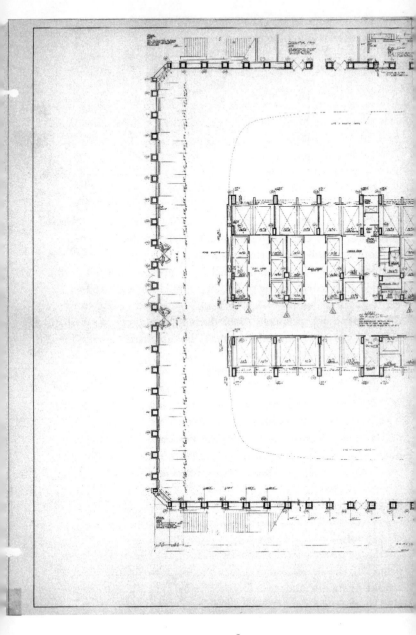

98

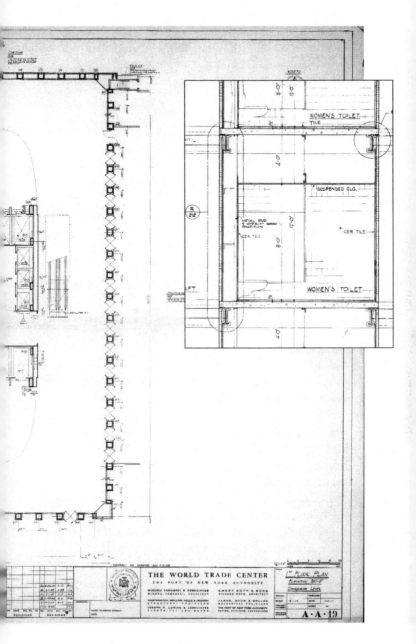

Then I take a look at the handwritten message from one Joseph H. Solomon, the fourth name on the firm's letterhead, wishing Paul the best and concluding, "If you ever receive a commission to do a 110-story building in Australia, we will be happy to act as consultants or co-architects."

Thank you, Paul, thank you, Joseph, thank you, God.

WORLD PREMIERE

I am ready to try the false delivery to Barry's office. As it is just a drill, I decide to keep it simple: four or five hefty but manageable cardboard boxes should do the trick.

As always, I start with the garbage piles. Back home with a good selection of empty cardboard boxes and a bag full of junk, I manufacture a few packages, which I seal with wide brown strapping tape, the kind that is crisscrossed internally by nylon fibers and cannot be torn by hand. I call Annie to admire the professional-looking result.

Suddenly, I have a nightmarish vision, a scene from those escape movies I'm so fond of: a uniformed guard approaches a group of prisoners pushing a cart, orders them to stop, and asks them to open one of their bundles; upon their refusal, he plunges in his bayonet.

"If they ask us, we have to be able to open the boxes and show what's inside!" I say, tearing open the boxes with a razor blade and pouring their contents back in the garbage bag. Annie shakes her head in disbelief at such idiotic paranoia.

When I share my worries with JP, and insist upon borrowing a dolly full of reams of Xerox paper from his store, he also thinks I'm ridiculous, but he complies. The new boxes I fashion and seal with regular tape satisfy me: they are guardproof.

Twice I must push back the delivery date, because twice the Americans announce at the eleventh hour that they won't be able to make it.

Finally it's the day. Definitely. A time of 1 p.m. is confirmed.

No. Donald calls, he'll be here at 2:00.

He calls again. Scratch that! Make it 2:30.

At 2:25, Chester calls. "Sorry, I won't make it before three-thirty."

I know that Barry's office closes at 4:45.

At 4:25 p.m., our rented van heads down the ramp beneath the towers. It's a world premiere! JP drives. Donald and I, seated on the floor in the back, will play underpaid delivery boys, languidly pushing our dollies. Chester, in the front seat, will act as the boss. Barry is at his desk on the 82nd floor of the south tower and will not move until we show up. His phone number is on our delivery slip—modeled on a form from JP's store—in case a security employee wishes to check with the recipient.

In the security booth at the bottom of the ramp, the guard looks up from his newspaper and frowns in disdain at the paperwork JP shoves under his nose.

"Delivery, south tower," announces JP, not gracing the man with a look.

The guard does not even answer, but points his chin toward a loading dock at the end of a tunnel.

When I get out of the van, I see the word POLICE written in large white letters, twenty feet away from me. So this is the famous precinct under the towers that I've heard so much about for so long.

There's only one problem: we can't use our dollies to unload. The floor of our van is lower than the loading dock. I'll have to check on that prior to renting a truck for the coup.

JP slams the doors and drives away as planned, leaving Donald, Chester, and me with the boxes. Keeping my head down to avoid being recognized, I cannot observe the landscape as much as I want. Before I know it, we're in a freight elevator operated by a gum-chewing WTC employee who hears Chester say "Eighty-two!" and does not even bother to check our delivery papers.

The freight cage has no ceiling. Above my head, I watch each of the dim lights separating the floors pass me by—another world premiere—and bite my lips, so not to reveal my huge smile.

On the 82nd floor, we roll our merchandise to Barry's office. He signs our slips, does not so much as wink at me—I like that—and with pride, like an extra on a movie shoot who's been granted his first line of dialogue, hands the papers back to Chester, saying with impeccable Shakespearean delivery, "There you go! Thank you. I'll take it from here."

DIRTY LAUNDRY

I seldom use the word "fun," but this afternoon, it describes my mission. For once, I won't be covered in sweat, climbing for hours inside the towers; instead, festively dressed in white for a change, I stroll to the south tower lobby, open a forbidden door, and let gravity pull me down the stairs. Feeling carefree and innocent— I'm only looking for a bathroom, after all—I wander deep inside the basement's levels.

Soon I find what I'm looking for.

Standing in front of the loading platform, I pull out my measuring tape. To my right, the door of the police station opens and the chief leans out. He lights a cigar and distractedly sets his eyes on me. No measuring tape today, let's go!

But not before a sudden instinct makes me lean forward and press my chest against the sharp edge of the platform. Waving at an imaginary fellow at the other end of the loading alley, I shout, ". . . and make sure you tell Pierre!" all the while discreetly rubbing my chest left and right against the edge to imprint a line onto my shirt.

Outside, I measure from the dirty line on my chest to the bottom of my shoes: 4 feet exactly.

Back home, while I repeatedly wash the white shirt, unable to completely erase its grease-and-rust mark, the perfectionist in me can't help critiquing the choice of the name Pierre. Joe or Charlie would have been better.

A postcard with two lines, a thirty-second phone call—since Jean-Louis's departure, I have been informing him of the ups and downs of the coup, but today I start a long letter. Today, once and for all, I decide when to walk.

Flipping through my French datebook, which lists the saints' days, I notice I have already moved the date eleven times. I erase the latest entry, August 1, as boring and too soon. I like the seventh, it has a ring to it. The day before—when we'll be sneaking in with the equipment—reads: "Mardi 6 Août 1974, Transfiguration." I do not know what the name means in the iconography of Christianity, yet when I imagine entering the dark viscera of WTC, emerging from its crown, hanging a wire in total darkness, and, sometime later, appearing flooded with light, balanced atop the world, I find *transfiguration* a fitting epithet.

"The walk is August 7, in exactly three weeks . . . ," the letter begins.

The outcome of the false delivery; the fact that Barry found a large hiding place on his floor for men and equipment; the evidence that such a place must exist on the 82nd floor of the other tower; the simplicity of hiding there until nightfall, of using the stairs to hoist peacefully, one floor at a time, half a ton of equipment to the roof—all the heavy stuff goes with me in the south tower . . . Everything, I write everything to Jean-Louis.

Following the main lines of the new plan, I cover every detail of the rigging. I note each move Jean-Louis will have to make. I draw each knot he'll have to tie. I list every tool he'll need.

In conclusion, I compose a French-English lexicon of useful terms and advise my friend to copy it onto an index card he'll slip into his pocket. That way, he'll be able to communicate with his American accomplice.

The letter runs to twenty-one pages; it takes me four days.

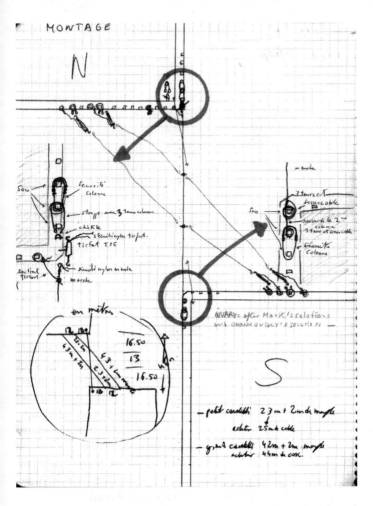

I reread the missive again and again, each time adding details and sketches and making corrections.

Before I lick the envelope, I can't resist going through the letter one last time. I'm particularly fond of the lexicon, which, besides *pull, push, lift, over there, right here*, also translates, *Be careful, it's going to slide! Hold on, be quiet, I heard something!* and, in an eerie premonition, *Don't give up!*

Four days without sticking my nose out of the house, four days reduced to eating yogurt and smelling the cat piss of Annie's protégés!

DUSTIN HOFFMAN

A woman in the front row attempts to strike up a conversation with me as I am passing my hat after my performance outside the Metropolitan Museum of Art. She's a casting director, working on a project with Dustin Hoffman.

I mime "not interested" and pass. She trots after the hat to drop in her business card. I pick up the card, smell it, bury it in my pocket, and, lifting one eyebrow, present the hat to her. She throws in a dollar.

Much later I remember the card. I call.

On the top floor of a Madison Avenue skyscraper, I am invited into a comfortable wood-paneled office and left alone.

I press my nose to the window, admiring the view from fifty stories up. Hoffman comes in and holds out his hand to me, but lost in the void, I make him wait before shaking his. "Hey, it's pretty nice up here!" I say.

The actor is relaxed and smiling. He offers me some wine, then explains that he is directing a theatrical production having to do with circus arts, and because his collaborators admired my street-performing, he wanted to meet me, and he proposes to hire me for . . .

Almost from the beginning I lose interest, and the corky young wine annoys my palate. "I'm not only a street-juggler, I'm also a high wire walker, look!" I say, flipping the pages of the huge photo album I brought with me. "See? Here in Paris, here in Sydney, all without permission!"

I explain I cannot consider his offer because I'm busy working on a surprise high wire walk.

He asks where, when.

"Oh, that I can't tell. It's a secret! I'm going to put a wire without permission between two buildings, somewhere in New York City!"

"Well, I can tell you a great place to put a wire," says the actor, beaming.

"Where?"

"The World Trade Center!"

"You mean those two big towers all the way downtown? Brilliant idea!" I comment, discreetly pouring my wine into a crystal vase full of roses when the actor is not looking.

On my way to the door, I ask if he would like to come to the show.

"Oh, absolutely!" he replies, frowning in puzzlement at the purple water in the vase.

I tell him that once the cable is up and I'm ready to walk, I'll have accomplices calling the press and then a list of friends. I offer to add him to the list.

"Yes, please, that would be nice."

"But it's possible they'll call you at six a.m."

"It doesn't matter. I want to be on the list! I want to be on the list!" the actor says with amused disbelief, giving me his phone number.

ALBERT

Usually, when I decide to gather everyone at West 22nd Street to rehearse the coup, the Americans arrive late or cancel at the last moment. When I do manage to assemble everyone, invariably Donald interrupts by playing the piano. He insists that I add padding to the equipment going to the roof, so that he and his friend won't hurt their shoulders. And Chester has been growing increasingly distant.

Today, he announces he is no longer able to help me in the towers.

Panic-stricken, I call Jean-Louis, who has someone else in mind.

But the Americans have a friend to replace Chester: someone brisk and agile who has worked on a boat, someone who knows all kinds of knots.

They've told him everything!

My first meeting with Albert—a nimble young man with short black curls and moustache, wearing glasses—leaves me with an intuition of distrust. I like his intelligence and seriousness, I sense he can follow any adventure, get out of any trap, and he shows me a few knots I'm not familiar with; but his enthusiasm is guarded and he chooses his words as he speaks.

Albert is also a photographer, and he offers to shoot the walk as well as help with the rigging. I explain that Jean-Louis is to be the exclusive photographer of the coup, and Annie insists that Albert must not take any pictures, even as souvenirs, "Or else it's better you're not part of the coup at all!" I'm flabbergasted at Annie's ultimatum—a potential disaster, so close to the walk. But Albert answers in a detached tone, "Fine, fine . . . I don't give a shit about photographs."

JEAN-FRANÇOIS

Jean-Louis calls from Paris. "How about that young guy who helped us at Notre-Dame?"

I don't have the faintest idea who he's talking about.

"Oh come on, Philippe, don't be disgusting. You know, Jean-François—he saved your life!" Jean-Louis reminds me that Jean-François had agreed to help at Notre-Dame only if he were sure to be freed in the morning in time to play an important tennis match. I had, of course, promised him the moon. An exhausted and dirty Jean-François had showed up on the court very late—and won.

"Yeah, it vaguely rings a bell," I say unenthusiastically, "but it isn't necessary to get anyone else since I have enlisted this genius new guy who has already accomplished his first mission:

he spent the night in the south eighty-second-floor hiding place and brought back a complete activity report, and . . . "

Jean-Louis hangs up on me and places another call.

In an isolated hamlet in the south of France, the phone rings thirty times in a tiny house surrounded by fig trees. A young feminine voice puts the caller on hold.

The girl runs after her boyfriend, who has gone up a brook looking for pebbles. Jean-François's childish silhouette, perfectly proportioned, bare-chested and barefoot, is kneeling on a rock. His baby face, framed by thick, disheveled golden locks, wears a beatific smile. Clutching a handful of shiny pebbles, he is admiring a butterfly delicately perched on his knuckles.

"Jean-François, quick, someone is calling from Paris!"

"*Allo*? Ah, my dear Jean-Louis! How is life treating you? And to what do I owe the pleasure of . . . New York? How? . . . Oh, you'll arrange it . . . Yes, in Paris. Day after tomorrow. Bye!— Oh, Jean-Louis? . . . Would you be kind enough to inform me of what is going on? . . . Without permission, I see . . . And you're looking for an uncomplaining sherpa who is ready to spend some time in jail . . ."

Jean-François hangs up, smiling.

"What was so urgent?" worries his girlfriend.

"Oh, nothing," he answers calmly. "I have to leave for a few days."

"Where are you going?"

"Mmm, to New York!"

Security is improving at WTC.

Barry calls to tell me that from now on every employee must carry an identification card: he received his today. "Would you by any chance be interested in"—he clears his throat and lowers his voice—"seeing it?"

Only minutes later—I was at One Hudson Street, building a table for Jim—I appear in front of a dumbfounded Barry. I grab the I.D. from his hands and rush home to study the document.

The thing is too professionally done. I don't stand a chance. Plus, I left my counterfeiting kit in Paris. Nonetheless, I give it a try. By midnight, all my replicas end up in the wastebasket, from which I retrieve them a moment later to throw them in the fire.

But what about, at the time of the coup, providing the group with an identification card of its own?

Back to the drawing board. I open the Yellow Pages at random and point at a name: Fisher. I design a logo for the nonexistent Fisher Company, which specializes in electrified fences and roofing.

By 3 a.m., the result is awful. And I don't have the time for that!

In the morning, Jim saves the day. He has a friend—a graphic designer.

I rush my seven lousy I.D.s to the expert, satisfy him with a haphazard explanation and quite excitedly offer my help. He is a craftsman, accustomed to working alone, and he does not need my agitation. "Take a walk instead," he advises.

In the evening, I pick up the improved documents: they're perfect.

Very nicely, the man offers to fill in the names and expiration dates, adding that his wife is an excellent typist.

Instantly, I come up with fake names.

By now, the woman has put the first card in the typewriter.

"Stop!" I shout. I ask her to try first on a piece of paper. With a lovely smile, she assures me that it is not a problem for her to type a few words accurately. After all, she's a professional typist, she says, placing her fingers back on the keyboard.

I jump up and pull the card from the machine, fumbling apologies. These documents are so important to me that I'm not willing to take any risk, I explain. And since there is no time to make a new batch, I prefer to find a typewriter and do it myself.

Yielding with grace to my paranoia, the woman complies: on a separate sheet, she types the seven names and dates in less than thirty seconds, rips out the paper, and hands it to me with a smile of superiority.

I point out the three typos.

The champion speed-typist—on the verge of tears, and in the most deadly silence—types each entry with one trembling finger, one letter at a time, on the precious cards.

I heap a profusion of thanks and apologies on the carpet and flee with my treasures.

Five days before the arrival of Jean-Louis and Jean-François in Boston—the only available flight on such short notice—I organize a dress rehearsal.

Organize? Not really.

To Albert and Donald, I transmit my wishes: we need to spend a few hours out of New York, in complete privacy, on a secluded flat piece of solid land bordered by a few trees, so that I can try out the equipment and show them the rigging sequence. They say they'll organize it, no problem.

No problem? Not really.

Albert is great. He gets hold of a car. He finds a friend who has property in upstate New York, "just as you described and only two hours away." He assures me he knows how to get there.

By 10 a.m., the trunk of the vehicle is crammed with so much equipment it sinks to the ground. When Albert puts the car in gear, with Annie and me in the back and Donald in the front, I hear metal scraping beneath us, but keep quiet.

We get lost, well . . . several times.

And the maps, well . . . they're the wrong maps.

But by noon, we're back on track.

Except noon is . . . "Lunchtime!" Donald insists on stopping somewhere: "We can't work on empty stomachs."

"No, we certainly can't," I sigh in misery.

And what can I say when Albert detours from the main road to salute some relatives he has not seen for a while, saying, "It'll only take a minute"?

Nothing, I say nothing.

It is not until the moment when daylight hesitates to bring on the evening that we drive through a little wood and find ourselves in a minuscule fenced-in lot.

From left to right: a small geodesic dome stands near a muddy embankment leaning into a murky pond holding a cloud of mosquitoes. The whole area is lined with tall reeds and shrubs: not a single tree.

"This is it!" says Albert triumphantly, gesturing toward what I would call an inclined swamp, much too small for my purpose.

Take away the time to greet Albert's friend, the time to comment on the beautiful property, the time to unload the equipment, and it is getting dark. I barely have time to unroll the walk-cable away from the mud, to attach the two cavalettis to it, to anchor the cable to the bushes, and to— No, there's no room for laying out the second cavaletti line, and nowhere to anchor it. As the Tirfor lifts the damn installation off the ground, a semiobscurity falls upon us and it starts to drizzle.

Donald and Albert help like underpaid marionettes. There is no time for me to explain anything. Albert invades my rigging with quick knotting demonstrations—he wants to show off his knowledge—while the landowner scrupulously shoots the entire episode on video.

So much for privacy!

It is pitch-black and raining hard when I finish assembling the balancing pole and am ready to step on the very loose wire.

Out of rage, I throw myself on the wire, do a forward somersault, and finish with two nocturnal backward rolls, all perfectly in line. "It has been four months since you set foot on a cable," remarks Annie.

The mud, the darkness, and the rain make the teardown a debacle and chase us back to New York City. The whole expedition has served absolutely no purpose.

Filled with bitterness and despair, I shrink my exhausted, wet, and freezing body into the fetal position in the backseat, with Annie's arms acting as a human safety belt. Eyes tightly closed, teeth tightly clenched, I remind myself, one after the other, of all the elements of past preparations, which are to me—now on the verge of tears—so many proofs that the coup will not happen.

Americans slouch all evening in front of their television sets, absorbed by a Movie of the Week or a baseball game. Not I.

I crave only a specific segment of the news: the weather. It's on almost every channel. It's short.

Sometimes I cannot find it.

Sometimes I just miss it.

I never understand it.

I know it concludes with the five-day forecast, a fast-paced, off-camera monologue illustrated by five vertical columns clearly showing each day's expected conditions.

The commentary is too rapid for me to catch a single word. And the captions—well, I try to make sense of temperature and wind speed, but degrees Fahrenheit and miles per hour still confuse me, plus I've always been uneasy with east and west. (Don't laugh, I still mix them up.)

When I try to jot down the figures, the chart is gone before I copy the first column.

So here I am, just days before the walk, often till two in the morning, attempting to make sense of the elements upon which my life depends.

Who believes that?

As if the weather—or anything, or anyone—could stop me now!

NOBODY'S FAULT

I have those rare moments when I contemplate the equipment. They are precious to me. I let my hands, my eyes distractedly brush by, surveying the tools of the trade. Call it technical daydreaming: a way for me to show appreciation for the craftsman's tools, sometimes subconsciously pursuing a solution, considering an improvement, foreseeing the perfect rigging, imagining the outcome, being satisfied.

Take the fishing-line spool, for example. It will link the flying arrow to the next line. It will perform the most important phase of the rigging: joining, for the first time, the ever-separated twin towers. It will allow me to pass the cable. Look how cleverly the—

"*What!?*" I scream in disbelief, as the cats run for cover.

I have just noticed that the 300 feet of transparent thread have been wound the wrong way on the spool. The arrow would have been brought to a halt by the drag! I pay out the fishing line and respool it, recalling that it was Paul who proudly volunteered for the task.

It's nobody's fault. I should be the one checking and rechecking everything.

Hypnotized by the monotonous process of coiling, I drift back into a state of contemplation. I imagine Jean-Louis missing the first shot. I see the arrow being pulled back up to the roof, I hear it bang against the windows at each floor, I watch the guard's response . . .

Even if my friend retrieves the arrow safely, he won't have the hour it takes to respool. Am I seeing it all wrong? Should we have two arrows, three bows, four extra spools, five balancing poles? I dismiss such absurdity. The coup relies less on equipment than on knowledge, on skills, on tenacity, and yes, on faith.

I believe Jean-Louis has trained properly; he'll shoot the arrow like a Zen master.

VIPs

SUNDAY, AUGUST 4, 1974

Worried about being even a minute late, I take one of the first trains to Boston. I won't let anyone know how early I arrive at the airport; I would have time to install a long red carpet for my VIP friends.

When it is announced that the flight from Paris is delayed, I laugh. And wait.

Finally, here comes Jean-Louis—in his disguise for the coup, a brown three-piece suit.

And here comes . . . Jean-François! I recognize him by his gentle smile. With his frayed pastel-blue pants rolled to midcalf, his Tunisian sandals, and an off-white shirt open to the navel, sleeves rolled to midbicep, he looks like an aborigine who missed his connection to Teti'aroa.

I welcome my friends in my arms.

During the train ride to Manhattan, Jean-Louis hands me an orange box. Inside, a collection of 8-by-10 photographs of WTC stairways and doors, arranged in order of his descent with Annie two months ago, awaits my admiration. I congratulate him on the quality of the prints.

Do I have a surprise for him? Oh yes, I say. I tell of the fake I.D.s, New Paltz, the blueprints.

Despite my show of enthusiasm and the fanfare with which I introduce each story, Jean-Louis turns somber. He asks me a few questions and understands he is not about to get the answers he expected.

We're about to argue again. Hell, it's war!

Noting that the coup is still not organized, Jean-Louis proposes changing all my plans. As soon as we enter the hiding places on our respective 82nd floors—allowing for a brief respite to regroup—we should go to the stairs and climb all the way to the 110th floors. Then we wait until nightfall to go up to the roof. The stairs are the area where we're most likely to be caught, he argues. Better to climb in broad daylight when the offices are open, when it's normal to meet people there.

"Yes," I say, "but since in broad daylight we're almost sure to meet people in the stairways, it increases the chances of getting caught."

"But at night, if we get accosted, we have no excuse for being there. And at night, there's a ninety percent chance that person will be a guard wanting to know what's going on."

"But by day, when we're sure to pass a whole bunch of people, there's going to be somebody asking us where we're going."

"Shit, Philippe! Don't tell me you don't know what to say to that person! In broad daylight, you say, I don't know . . . You say you're going to such and such office, you've got to see so and so . . . But at night, what are you going to say? And if you are caught during the day, you have plenty of time to try again. But at night—you're caught, you're dead."

The argument is never-ending. Jean-François, smiling across from us, follows the bout as if it were a Ping-Pong match, turning his head left and right.

The first stop in Manhattan is to see Albert. Like me, Jean-Louis instinctively mistrusts his apparent humorlessness, and surely Albert picks up on his mistrust.

At home, the happy reunion between Annie and the two heroes of the day does not postpone our duel for long. Jean-Louis tries to lift one piece of equipment after another and criticizes my being satisfied with a hiding place so far from the roof. "Do you really see yourself carrying all this, extremely fast and silently, from the eighty-second floor to the hundred and tenth?"

"You've got a better solution?" I ask ferociously.

"It was *your* job to find the solutions—not mine! The only reason I'm back is you swore everything was ready this time. Except, big surprise, we're in exactly the same mud as before. We're not one hair further. To the point that I—I don't even know if—I don't know if I'm interested in throwing myself into a suicide operation!"

I disappear for a while into the bedroom, trying to catch my breath, trying to catch my mind; Annie tries as well. But each time I come out of the bedroom the absurd battle continues. Jean-François is no longer smiling, although my repeated withdrawals into the bedroom to rage and emergences to fight must belong to the repertoire of early comic cinema.

MONDAY, AUGUST 5

Jean-Louis and I clash until 5 a.m., when our bodies collapse in unison on the sofa—another funny tableau, if only we had the good humor to appreciate it.

Two hours later, I wake up in the bedroom. I don't know how I got there.

I escape the sleepy apartment to meet JP, who is helping me rent the truck. I painstakingly choose one with a loading platform exactly 4 feet off the ground.

I return home at ten to a houseful of laughter. It quiets down when Albert and Donald stop by, uninvited, to share a quick breakfast with us. I see the way Jean-Louis sizes up Donald's personality with a glance—and I can almost read his verdict in the air: "Another of your great finds, bravo!"

By 11 a.m., it's time to go to JP's store for the I.D. pictures. We line up to pose one by one in front of a dirty white sheet as JP professionally clicks away and yells "Next!" after each flash.

Next, Albert brings us to a giant store close to the World Trade Center. Brilliant! They have everything from washed-out T-shirts and second-hand pants for the delivery crew to an impeccable businessman's outfit for Albert. Except that Albert chooses the most expensive (and ugliest) three-piece suit, and then adds to the bill an ugly tie and an ugly expensive shirt and comes back for an ugly pair of socks.

"Consider yourself lucky he has his own shoes, your *genius* accomplice!" whispers Jean-Louis.

I let the Americans go, reminding them there is a final rehearsal meeting at 9 p.m. at West 22nd Street.

Back at the house, Jean-Louis and I resume our argument.

Jean-Louis accuses me of having concentrated too much on the south tower, my tower; he is furious to have no intelligence about *his* 82nd-floor hiding place, in the north tower.

"But the hiding places are the same. They're *twin* towers!" I tease.

"Don't give me that bullshit! Did you go and check?"

I did, with Barry, and Albert scouted it before he spent the night in my tower, but that doesn't appease Jean-Louis.

"Yeah? Then you can tell me how to go from my hiding place to the roof."

"Of course! It's the same as in my tower! There's a staircase—"

"That staircase, you tried it? Can you tell me if I have to go left or right when I get out of the hiding place? Can you tell me which corridor I have to take and which door I have to open at the end of it? Can you tell me how many steps there are to the first landing, or how many landings there are to the summit? Can you show me on one of your fabulous blueprints where it opens out to the roof? And what about the guards? Do you know how many there are, on which floor they sit? When they change shifts?"

I am speechless.

"Okay. You know I'm here for four days only! Go and see right now!"

"But I can't!" I say in despair, explaining briefly my brush with the press and my innumerable visits.

Annie saves the day. She'll go with Jean-François. They'll come back with information.

"A naive French tourist couple going to the top to take a snapshot of the city, that's it! It's three-thirty. Quick! Go! Go! Go!" I applaud.

Jean-Louis has the bright idea of waiting for their return before reopening hostilities, while I find an activity in tune with my mood. I go to the garden with four newly purchased helmets and proceed to "age" them by kicking them in a furious soccer game and dragging them back and forth on the concrete slab and brick walls. Annie and Jean-François are back at 7 p.m., exhausted but victorious.

Jean-Louis gets most of his answers, but the fresh information reignites his battles with me. Before long, he's repeating his ultimatum: either I do things as he says, or he's out.

Annie wants me to reason with him, but I decide otherwise. I can't afford to lose him, so I'm going to agree with him. And after the coup, I'll never see him, I'll never talk to him again.

I walk to Jean-Louis and conclude softly, looking at the carpet to avoid his eyes, "Okay, let's climb by daylight. Let's do things your way."

He smiles. "Let's start packing."

At 9 p.m., Albert shows up for the briefing. He frowns at the alterations in the plan and starts challenging them one by one. Clearly he does not appreciate Jean-Louis's power.

Two hours late, Donald arrives from one of his concerts, accompanied by Chester. They're both drunk and stoned, and after Donald goes to the keyboard and launches into his longest song, there's not much of a briefing. Jean-Louis fumes and looks at me with disdain.

Shortly after midnight, the Americans leave. Jean-Louis helps me tag the equipment, blue for north tower, red for south, and we continue to prepare, and—the slightest detail becoming an issue —to argue.

THE COFFIN

TUESDAY, AUGUST 6, 1974
4 A.M.

Everything is ready. Everyone is asleep except me.

I, exhausted, disgusted, contemplate the moon mocking me.

I go and wake Annie. "We just fought like hell again. He refuses to take with him the wood to protect the beam. He keeps telling me, 'If you don't like it, find somebody else!' "

"You're not going to change Jean-Louis. It's almost five a.m., go to sleep."

"No, but you know what? I don't give a shit if Jean-Louis leaves. I can do it by myself!" I whisper in a rattle, "Actually, that's what I want. That's what I'm gonna do. I'm gonna do it all by myself. I need nobody."

I collapse on the mattress.

Minutes later, I spring up: "Shit! I forgot to nail the crate holding the cable!"

The wee-hour mist finds me in my underwear, the cold concrete of the yard digging into my naked knees as I frantically drive steel points into the crate, reluctantly imprisoning my friend the wire in its coffin. My hammering, or perhaps my screaming when I hit my fingers, brings a few irate neighbors to their windows.

6 A.M

I rest on the crate for a moment, my mind wandering, then rush back inside and wake Annie again. "Annie, you know . . . This whole thing is madness! It's true, nothing is organized! I know what's gonna happen! You want to know what's gonna happen? What's gonna happen is"—my voice takes a strange tone, I'm shaking with fatigue, I'm shivering with insanity—"we're going to drive down the ramp, we're going to unload, and there, right

there, we're going to get caught. I'm sure of that. I'm certain. It's a suicide. An absolute suicide."

Annie whispers back: "If you don't believe in it, why go for it? It's stupid to start a coup when you're sure to get caught!"

"No! I have to do it. I don't give a shit if I am caught; let them catch me! I prefer to be thrown in jail than not to try."

Annie buries herself under the sheets. Once again, I begin to review mentally every detail of the operation, but almost instantly I collapse, and this time I steal half an hour of sleep.

I wake up screaming at Annie: "Shit! I asked you to wake me up at eight. It's eight-thirteen!"

THE CARROTS ARE COOKED

TUESDAY AUGUST 6, 1974
8:15 A.M.

Infuriated, I run around the apartment and the garden. I come back in the bedroom shouting, "Annie! The pants aren't dry! I told you! I knew they wouldn't be dry!" Annie attempts to remind me that the rendezvous is at noon and the delivery is planned for 1:30 p.m. I'm not listening. I snatch the pants from the clothesline and arrange them to roast in front of the open oven, which I've set to 500 degrees Fahrenheit.

I am relentless. "What about something to eat—anything! And the black turtleneck sweater for the walk! I asked you— There's a hole, look! Do it right now! But make sure you put it back in the bag, in the second pocket, under my slippers! You won't forget to put it back?"

"No, I won't forget to put it back." Annie weighs each word.

Oblivious to my bad mood, Jean-Louis organizes his photographer's attaché case, checking his cameras with the professional dexterity of a marine assembling his M-16. Jean-François is in the garden conversing with the cats.

From now on, without consulting me, time accelerates.

11 A.M.
The bell rings. "*Qui c'est?*" I scream into the rusty intercom, forgetting to speak English. It's Jim—so sweet of him to arrive early. The room shines with his conviviality and good mood. He asks everyone, "Can I help?"

NOON
JP arrives exactly on time, munching a Granny Smith apple. "The truck is parked right in front!" he booms, leaning on the coffee table to fill out and sign the delivery forms.

1 P.M.
Albert arrives an hour late, grim as ever. No comments from anyone. Now we are all waiting for Donald.

Jean-Louis and I have one last quarrel: he wants water for our flasks, I want orange juice. Annie overrules us. She fills the containers with water and discreetly adds some fresh lemon juice and a teaspoon of sugar. She then prepares a gigantic salad.

"We'll lose time eating that!" I mutter, forgetting that I had asked her to feed us.

1:20 P.M.
Donald is finally here. No comments.

We all help to load the truck.

The huge empty crate goes first, mounted on a dolly. We fill it with most of the equipment and I nail the lid shut—without the wheels, not even six men could move such a load. Next comes the cylinder with the disassembled balancing pole, almost too heavy for one person. Equally as cumbersome is the cardboard box containing the Tirfor. The walk-cable in its coffin goes next, so heavy it needs a separate dolly.

Jean-Louis and Albert in their suits will enter the north tower with what they are carrying now. Jean-Louis holds the roll of blueprints, which contains the bow in two parts and its single arrow, and the oversized attaché case I hope will pass as a businessman's. It contains his photographic equipment, quite a few tools, and the loaded 16mm movie camera rented for the occasion. The case is so heavy that it is hard to carry without leaning to one side. Albert will carry an even bigger but lighter case, and he insists upon keeping on his shoulder a little travel pouch. "My personal things," he says.

We lock the truck. We go back inside the house. We make sure nothing has been forgotten. We put on our I.D.s.

"The carrots are cooked!" I remark to myself, aloud.

JP lifts an eyebrow, knowing we French make large use of expressions related to cooking. "The Americans say, 'The die is cast,' " he comments.

"Well, the carrots are cooked, my friend. If we wait any longer, they'll be mushy!" I quip, as Annie forces a plate onto everyone's lap and orders, "Let's eat!"

1:30P.M.
I see a silent tension setting in, but that's me.

PHILIPPE IS GOING TO DIE

In Germany, Francis Brunn knows that today is the day of the coup, and so does his Russian wife, Sasha.

They talk and talk about it, grabbing from each other's hands the telegram I have sent: WEDNESDAY AUGUST 7. IN THE MORNING. PP. Francis believes I will succeed, or be arrested during the rigging. Sasha is convinced I will succeed, by which she means I'll rig the wire, I'll get on it, and—it's written in her heart—I'll die.

She insists on saving her friend's life.
They argue.
She wins.

At 7:30 p.m., she picks up the phone. It is 1:30 in the afternoon in New York. She's dialing the cops. Her intention is not to reveal my name nor to explain what she knows is happening; it's just to warn them that something alarming is going to happen at the twin towers, probably on the rooftops, and to urge them to keep watch.

She can't get through.

She tries the numbers for WTC security, for the Port Authority police.

It rings and rings, but she can't reach anyone. Is it the renowned antiquity of the European telephone network, or is it still lunchtime in New York?

She tries again.

Wrong numbers, wrong connections . . .

In the back lot of Circus Sarrasani, a cold fog surrounds the artists' trailers as moonlight reveals the tent's canvas, another night descending. That's always when the giraffe rattles her chains, knowing her dinner is coming soon.

Sasha and Francis should really go to sleep.

They have a matinee tomorrow.

And so do I.

THE PLAN

Forgetting to eat, I create exasperation by reciting aloud once more the expected course of events:

Barry is at his desk, ready to answer the telephone.

We drive Jim home. He stays by his phone as well, ready to cover us by impersonating the receptionist of the Fisher Company.

The truck stops a hundred yards before the ramp. Jean-Louis and Annie jump out and take their posts on the sidewalk by the north tower's entrance.

JP drives the truck underneath the towers.

JP, Jean-François, Albert, Donald, and I unload.

When we reach the freight elevators serving the south tower, JP chats with the operator. Albert helps if necessary. Donald, Jean-François, and I are delivery boys, saying nothing. Jean-François and I in particular don't say a word from beginning to end of the delivery—and I hide my features as much as I can so no one recognizes me.

When we're inside the elevator, JP leaves us; he drives up the ramp and parks the truck in front of Jean-Louis and Annie. Annie rushes to Barry's office and waits.

Meanwhile, inside the freight elevator, Albert starts a conversation with the operator to convince him not to wait for us after we unload at the 82nd floor.

We unload at 82. Jean-François, Donald, and I push the dollies to Barry's office while Albert and the operator go back down by the elevator.

Albert rushes by foot from the basement to the street where the truck is parked. Inside the truck, he takes off his deliveryman clothes and puts on his businessman suit as fast as possible.

Upstairs, Barry escorts me, Jean-François, and Donald to the hiding place, then returns swiftly to his office, where Annie is waiting for him.

In the hiding place, we stay invisible and quiet until 6:30, when the guard in the nearby stairwell changes post. We open the crates and dash upstairs. We wait just beneath the roof, hiding where we can with the equipment until night comes. As soon as it's dark, we go up to the roof.

Jean-Louis and Albert are at the truck, waiting for Barry.

Barry goes down as fast as he can, using the elevators; he is led by Annie, who knows where the truck is parked.

Barry escorts Jean-Louis and Albert with their luggage to the other hiding place, on the 82nd floor of the north tower, and then goes back to his office in the south tower and waits there, just in case the phone rings. Meanwhile, JP returns the rental truck and Annie goes home.

Jean-Louis and Albert continue hiding until 6:30, then climb to just beneath the roof. When it's dark, they get on the roof.

We rig all night.

On the ground, Annie, Jim and Loretta, Barry and Linda, JP and Alicia gather at around 6 a.m. by the telephone booths across from the bank. Discreetly, not looking directly up, they watch for my first step. As soon as they see me get on the cable, Jim and Loretta get on the phones: Press first, then friends. In between calls, everyone cries out, gesticulating wildly and pointing at the wire: "Look, there's a wirewalker!"

Later, we all see each other at the apartment.

I do not believe a word of my litany. Nothing is going to happen as planned. All of us are going to get caught!

No one listens to me, anyway.

"Let's go!" Jean-Louis orders.

"ONE-OH-FOUR!"

We drive to WTC.

We drop Jean-Louis and Annie. I give Annie an effusive hug with passionate kisses, the kind that do not mean *au revoir* but *adieu*. She is terrified.

"Let's go," I say to JP.

We slow down at the entrance to the ramp.

In the back, I can feel the truck shifting from the horizontal of the street to the slant of the ramp. I'm the most fulfilled child on the planet.

The coup has started.

JP drives down the ramp, waves our fake delivery slips at the guard booth, and is directed to the south tower loading dock. He makes a U-turn at the platform and brings the back of the truck into perfect alignment with it. We unload the equipment on our dollies and push them to the bank of freight elevators, passing within fifteen feet of the bustling police station.

So far, everything is going according to plan.

At the elevator, dozens of men in overalls are maneuvering overloaded dollies. They hurry, they bump into each other and shout orders, they fight to fit inside whatever freight cab is next: it's a mob scene.

JP and Albert, papers in hand, go inquire what's going on. While Jean-François and Donald stay with the equipment, I retreat into a corner, looking at my shoes or scratching my forehead to hide my face.

What's going on? Today is moving day in the south tower! Several major moving companies have reserved the few freight elevators to deliver and install furniture for new tenants. The bad news is, there's no room for unscheduled puny deliveries like ours. "Come back another time!" roars the busy foreman.

A sorrowful JP is about to tell us to turn around and head back to the truck when I plant myself swiftly in front of my "boss" and give him my murderous-Roman-emperor look. I whisper, teeth clenched, my tone galvanic: "No, we stay! We wait!"

I roll the equipment out of the way of the frantic movers and arrange it in the smallest and neatest pile for the foreman to see. Jean-François, the sweetest of delivery boys, is helping most efficiently. Donald is faking it. We sit on the floor. I rest my elbows on my knees and hold my face in my hands as if I have a headache, peeking through my webbed fingers.

It takes a while for JP and Albert to catch the foreman taking a short break. I watch the three of them getting into a lively discussion. Ah, if only I had two hundred dollars in cash on me! The group is too far, I can't hear what is being said, but JP's body language is exemplary: calm, detached, but mildly insistent—he keeps pointing in the direction of the equipment, shrugging his shoulders. The man shakes his head repeatedly, but in the end he throws his arms in the air before hurrying back to his responsibilities.

My accomplices come back grinning, with the message, "Sure, wait all day if you feel like it, but don't count on it!" I congratulate them and instruct them to leave the foreman alone from now on, to tackle the elevator operators instead, without the foreman noticing. It's a delicate task: the operators work nonstop, and the foreman is everywhere.

I order Jean-François and Donald to sit by my side and disappear like me into invisibility. Head down, I keep watch, while telepathically urging the pile of equipment to reduce its volume. It doesn't.

JP is good. It's taken him two hours, but he's gotten friendly with one of the elevator guys.

Then a loud ring pierces our eardrums, a full thirty seconds. It's the end-of-the-day bell singing 4 p.m. "Everybody out!" shouts the foreman.

First miracle: the foreman walks up to us, considers our depressed forms and our insignificant load of goods, points to the elevators, and tells us with a sigh of mercy, "Okay, guys, but make it snappy!"

He grabs our papers and asks where we're headed. He points to an elevator: "Take that one." He gives our papers to the operator and orders: "Hey Jack, do me a favor, I swear it's your last trip: eighty-two."

We rush our dollies inside. The cabin is shaking. The operator shoves our papers between his teeth to free his hands. He grips the handle: "Let's go!" On the plywood wall above his head, I notice a partly erased pencil scribbling: 0–104.

Second miracle: not only does the operator happen to be JP's new friend, but he hasn't heard his foreman's order clearly.

"What floor?" he inquires.

Without thinking, I pounce on the extraordinary opportunity. Despite each parcel being clearly labeled "82nd floor," despite a bold "82nd" dangling three inches from the guy's eyes on the papers he's holding in his mouth, despite my intention not to utter a word or show my face during the delivery, I step on JP's feet and cough heavily to cover his loud "eighty-two." I look the operator right in the eyes and say without hesitation, "One-oh-four!"

"One-oh-four? But there's nothing up there! It's all empty!"

"We know, but we're bringing stuff for the electrified fence on the roof and some pieces for the antenna," I say, showing the balancing-pole package and trying to minimize my French accent. I pray that the man is ignorant that the antenna is being erected on the other tower.

"Whatever. Watch your hands!" warns the operator mechanically, hurling the cage upward with the most delightful squeaking I've ever heard.

The plan no longer exists. I've just saved Donald, Jean-François, and myself an exhausting expedition I always knew was doomed to fail.

At my feet, suffocating beneath thin wooden boards, 200 kilos of 22-millimeter cable lies coiled in slumber, a wild steel snake waiting to be set free. Above my head, the tiny square of light indicating the end of the shaft grows larger. Inside my skull, the thousand elements of a new plan bite one another in the face, like mad dogs. The floors pass by, the elevator accelerates, the noise is deafening.

Without moving my lips, I whisper to JP and Albert my improvised plan: as soon as we arrive at 104, while I direct the unloading, they'll convince the operator to abandon Donald, Jean-François, and me and take them back down.

"You think it'll work?" murmurs JP.

"We've got no choice, make it work!" I snap.

"One-oh-four!" yells the lift man.

JP and Albert are brilliant. They start a friendly chat with the man.

"Look, our guys have to bring all this stuff to storage. They've got to get their slips stamped. It's gonna take a while. Your shift is over and we've got another load downstairs to rush to Queens."

"Why don't we leave them here? They know their way down—it's not the first time they've been here."

The operator glances at his watch and shrugs. "Whatever. Watch your hands!" The elevator plunges into darkness.

Jean-François and I tear open the boxes and pry open the crates as fast as we can while Donald watches. Wearing our gloves and helmets, we rush silently up the six flights. Actually we rush one step at a time, resting—with time we don't have—every ten steps. The equipment is unbearably heavy.

A half hour later, I arrive with my troops on the 110th floor, just under the roof. I have hate in my heart for Donald, who is slow and complaining and shows signs of giving up.

I hear distant banging, nearby conversations, and the dying sound of power tools being switched off. It's quitting time, but the floor is not yet deserted. Workers seem to be coming our way. I scan the floor for the little staircase leading to the roof, but recent work has rendered the place foreign to me.

I start to panic. Ah! Here it is.

We drop our equipment against the stairwell. No time to hide it—I hear people coming down from the roof. I spy an immense green tarp in the middle of the floor. We run to it. No time to think. I lift the thick canvas; it's dark in there. I literally throw Jean-François under it. He screams. I throw myself in. I scream.

Third miracle: We've landed on a narrow I-beam overlooking three floors of emptiness—some kind of service elevator under construction that eluded my scouting.

"Donald! Quick! Get in!" But Donald needs more room, needs more time, needs more light; he asks if it's safe to step on this, to hold on to that . . .

Without premeditation, I take the step I've known was coming. "Donald, wait! I'm just thinking, we don't need three people up there, two is plenty. There's something more important for you to do. See the tarp behind me? Overlap the two ends so no opening is visible, then run tell the others we're already under the roof with all the equipment."

Who is more relieved, he or I?

I know rigging alone with Jean-François will be a task of Herculean proportions, but at least friendship, perseverance, and joy will float in the air.

Here we sit on an eight-inch-wide beam, facing each other, our feet in each other's crotches, our hands grasping the beam's thin edge behind us to keep our balance. Not an easy position to hold, no room to move, not much air to breathe, only darkness to watch. The tarp rests on our heads and bodies, so the slightest movement could betray us.

By now, it must be 4:30.

Our goal? To stay still and silent until night comes. We are trapped.

Do I know how many more miracles are in store for us?

Oh, I know. Many.

AN ETERNITY

Under the tarp, Jean-François and I are left to our immobility and our sight impairment.

For a while, eyes closed, I pay attention to the serene breathing of the tower and to the distant humming of the city. But soon I find myself galloping through memories of the adventure. I go to the dentist, I see my towers for the first time, I take my helicopter flight, I go see Francis and Papa Rudy, I do the Hundred Meters at Vary . . .

Time has no grasp in my thoughts, but suddenly I'm pulled from my reverie by the crackling of a walkie-talkie.

A guard is coming toward our hiding place. Has he seen the tarp move? He is getting closer. He reaches the tarp. I cannot see Jean-François, but I feel his legs go rigid.

God! The guard is leaning against a column, an inch from my shoulder. I hold my breath.

Is he waiting for us to give ourselves up? No. He is lighting a cigarette! He is so close I can hear the dry scratch of the match, the sulfur tip bursting into flame, and the man's breath as he exhales the first puff. Holding even my thoughts, I remain a statue for a long, long time. Then suddenly the guard is gone. Or has he fallen asleep right behind me? No, he's gone. I'm not sure.

To ease the torment, I return to my memories, the gold-and-mud years of dreaming, months of organizing. I encounter the magician at customs, I'm "arrested" on the roof, I taste despair, I look in vain for another site. From time to time, I return briefly to reality, trying to estimate how long it has been since we hurled ourselves under the tarp. Is it still daylight outside? What if the guard is still around? What if he is toying with us—comfortably sitting in his chair facing us, waiting for us to make the slightest sound, the slightest movement—before he pounces on us and arrests us? We must wait.

After an eternity, I can't keep myself in the past anymore. I need to know if the sky is getting darker.

With infinite precautions—I'm convinced the guard is still there—I pull a pencil from my shirt pocket (a process that, with the canvas resting on my wrist, must take ten minutes). I bring the sharp lead in contact with the heavy cotton canvas and, rolling the pencil back and forth between my fingers, slowly, gradually work the point between the tightly woven fibers of the tarp. I'm afraid if the point goes through the canvas all at once, it will create a tiny *plick*. Another ten minutes.

I remove the pencil and slowly bring one eye to the hole, but it is too small for me to see anything. My fingers creep back to my pocket in slow motion, to retrieve a fat ballpoint pen. By twisting its metal cone into the existing canvas hole, after an excruciating amount of time I manage to enlarge the pinhole into a quarter-inch porthole.

The hole is still too small to record anything with precision, but panning around I can make out a maze of beams, the familiar clutter of a floor under construction, a faraway broken panel revealing a patch of sky, and no silhouette of a guard. I do not—oh, how exasperating—do not see the sky becoming darker.

I retreat once again to the film of my memory. Where was I? Ah—Jean-Louis arrives. We fight, I fail. I start my "new organisation." I find Barry, I lose Barry. Annie's sandals, Annie's cats, Annie's tender understanding . . . I forget time for another eternity, until Jean-François breaks the spell by tapping his heels against my groin.

Transgressing our vow of silence for the first time, I whisper, annoyed but in the softest voice, "*Whaaaat?*" My friend wants to know when we're getting out. I let go an extremely faint and trailing, "*Shuuut uuup!*" and retire to my recollections.

I find Barry again, I visit the hiding place he discovered, I hunt for accomplices . . .

Such mental vagabondage must do away with a few hours, but I am still not rewarded with a dark sky. Instead, I get a sky wanting to become darker . . . and a terrifying ophthalmic migraine for stupidly having left my retina glued to the minuscule hole for so long: eyes open or closed, I see little accordions of bright silver floating around. Will this problem affect my equilibrium on the wire?

Why worry?

I dive back into the past for a long while until Jean-François hits me again. The immobility is torturing him, he must change position. I forbid him. He could fall; a shift in the canvas could alert a guard. He begs me to remove his shoes. I would kill to free my own feet. If only someone could see us, how absurd and grand: we spend probably half an hour untying each other's shoelaces and pulling off the four heavy construction boots, one by one, without perceptible movement, without a sound. The steel I-beam is still cutting through my butt, but what a relief to move my toes, and it's not completely unpleasant to have Jean-François's naked feet resting on my crotch.

It's still daylight; I go back to the story of my adventure. I make the phony I.D.s, take that pitiful trip to upstate New York . . .

Once more Jean-François interrupts, demanding to know if night has come. "No," I growl, in the lowest possible tone.

I'm at the point of Jean-Louis's most recent arrival and the discord that followed, when Jean-François is at it again: he wants to know what time it is. "How would I know?" I reply, fingering through my pants my sturdy pocket watch.

The exercise of pulling out the watch and bringing its face under the dim light emanating from the hole seems to occupy half an hour. I confess to Jean-François, "I've got a watch!" "Bastard!" he whispers back.

The ray of light is not wide enough to illuminate a whole numeral on the face of the watch. Slowly, I promenade each number under the light—Is that a 3? A 2?—until, guessing more than reading, I can tell what figure it is. It's my bad luck that at this moment, the two thin hands of the watch are far apart from each other, so I must chase them with my tiny fading spotlight across the face of the watch. When I see one hand, I lose the other, and they keep moving on their own! When I lose a number, it takes me a great deal of time to trap its shape and read it again. By now my pounding headache has me half blind.

No doubt, if I survive this ordeal, I'll give lectures on the infinitesimally small and the relativity of time.

An eternity after having pulled out the watch, I am victorious: "It is eight o'clock!" I share the news with Jean-François, who, aware of my struggle, replies, "Yeah, or twenty to twelve!"

Another triumph: through my minuscule porthole, the sky is decidedly turning dark. Soon, soon, this waiting will come to an end.

I rest my eyes and return to my story. But now I'm confused. Too many players, too many scenes—the film overlaps, then fades to black. Much time has passed. Why, when I decipher the watch again, does it read only 8:30?

From now on, each time I bounce out of the story, the pain is excruciating: my muscles are crushed by the steel, my eyes are burning, my head is exploding, immobility zigzags cramps all over my body, and my patience has evaporated. Jean-François is in similar agony.

Repeatedly, I nail the cable's crate shut. Over and over, I order "One-oh- four!" in a freight elevator that goes nowhere. I force the train of my memories to keep running, but the facts refuse to march past. Glued to the pinhole, glued to the pocket watch, listening to the pain, I count each second of each minute. An eternity, indifferent to us, calmly stacks them on the scaffold of time, until it is pitch-black outside and my watch reads nine o'clock.

To hell with precautions! Forgetting to whisper, I tell my friend to get out, to stay barefoot, and to grab with me the two linked coils of the enormously heavy walk-cable. I lift the canvas carefully, I look around. "Let's go!"

Stiff and fragile, we tiptoe in pain—but in complete silence—the twenty feet separating our hiding place from the ministaircase leading to the roof. At the base of the stairs, we put our hands on the coils—

Stop! We hear loud conversation coming from the roof, laughter, what sounds like the clash of beer bottles.

Terrified, we dash back to the hiding place.

There seems to be a party on the roof, probably a group of construction workers celebrating. How could this noisy group have brushed by us without our hearing? Could the tarp have muffled the sound so perfectly? Probably the happy gathering is illegal, and they tiptoed their way to the top. Did our guard play a part in that scheme? We were right to stay dead like stones. We cannot even share our bewilderment—we're back to strict immobility and muteness. For how long? Don't the gods take pity on us?

I am back to my thoughts, but no longer in the past. I think if the merrymakers up there decide to party through the night, there will be no dancing wirewalker in the morning. I liberate one ear from the tarp to track the faint coming and going sounds of the party. After an eternity it becomes quiet. Have they gone, as silently as they had come? To be safe, I force us to wait, still and silent, for another hour, our ultimate torment.

Gently lifting the canvas, I'm about to get out when a faint talking-and-laughing murmur reaches my ear and grows and grows and comes toward us.

I instantly replace the canvas over my head and freeze, hitting Jean-François in the groin with my feet. I had forgotten: there is always a time in a party when people calm down and fall silent. The happy procession passes very close to us, then moves away. The echo of footsteps fades from our floor.

Now the path should be clear. But what if . . . ?

For good measure, indifferent to our bodies' pain, their plea for motion, I order an extra quarter of an hour of dead stillness. Now, that is an eternity, and that you could call torture.

It's 9:45. I gather my strength. I concentrate.

With infinite precautions—I no longer trust my ears—we slide silently out of our cocoon. We stumble invisibly to the staircase. Each of us grabs and lifts a coil of the walk-cable—I don't know how, they're too heavy for a mule. In a mad, obstinate gesture, I pick up the bag full of cavaletti lines and add it to my load. Jean-François is six feet ahead of me, his legs trembling, and like prisoners chained to each other, we inch our way up, one step at a time.

On the third step, my heart stops.

In front of me, visible through the skeleton of the staircase, barely fifty feet away, leaning his elbows on a small table under a naked light bulb, a man in uniform is staring at me with semi-closed eyes. On the table, I see a large flashlight, a walkie-talkie, and a guard's cap.

I lean back to halt Jean-François's climb. If I stop him, he's going to look back. If he looks back, I'll give him the most dramatic glance, alerting him that a disaster is in the making, signaling with only my eyes, "Don't move, don't breathe, but keep gliding up, keep climbing, invisible and still!"

It's eerie, the guard has his eyes set on my person, but he does not seem to see me . . . as if his eyes were looking through my body. Maybe he's sleeping . . . with his eyes open? Maybe he's watching us and thinks we're a couple of workers earning overtime . . . without helmets or shoes? Maybe he's under the influence of some drug?

But Jean-François will not stop! On the contrary, he's pulling me to the roof. I resist. For an instant, we're playing a surreal tug-of-war . . . He wins!

Escaping the guard's field of vision has taken no longer than three seconds.

Slapped in the face by a fresh wind, and despite the enormous load, we noiselessly collapse on top of each other on the roof, like rag dolls. Jean-François victoriously whispers in my ear in the fastest French: "I had seen your silly guard long before you, but thought we better not stop, that's why I pulled you!"

I imagine what a ruckus we would have made if we had kept our shoes on. Another miracle!

A half miracle, actually . . . since we are now on the roof, barefoot, three hours late, with only the walk-cable and cavalettis in our possession while the rest of the equipment is kept hostage by a guard who might stand post all night, who might come up to the roof at any moment.

My instinct is to bring my friend to his knees, force his head down through the staircase opening, and order him to stay like that, upside down, keeping the guard under surveillance until he leaves and we can retrieve our equipment, or until he comes to the roof and I can . . .

I do exactly that.

Above a kneeling Jean-François, a concert of stars has started, just for me.

I know the coup is a failure. But I am happy to be on the roof, and I am insane.

BAD, BAD PANELS!

From my roof, I see three things.

But first I do something that cannot be done.

I wake up the walk-cable, flat asleep on the concrete. I make the two coils stand up and—I certainly don't have the strength—hoist a coil onto each shoulder. Unable to walk at all, I walk to the edge, where I let my cable be repossessed by the law of gravity as I collapse at his side, possessed by sheer delight. What I just did remains scientifically unproven, in the realm of the impossible.

The night is limpid, black, and blue.

I see, atop my tower, only the beams of aircraft beacons, sweeping with regularity, offering me useless and ephemeral shades of light.

I see, looking at the roof of the north tower, two shapes walking in the dark—not walking, sneaking. I know they are the silhouettes of Jean-Louis and Albert. What perfection, for the two crews to appear barely a half hour apart: this is a professional operation!

My joy is cut short by what I see next.

I see, under the dark forms of my friends moving slowly on the upper roof, aluminum panels on the crown of the building. Last time I checked, they covered a few slant columns near the southwest corner, but now they are bolted over most of the columns. (The construction workers should be congratulated on such fast progress.) The shiny gray skin has grown over most of the crown, leaving no place for the cavalettis to be anchored as planned—a disaster! Nothing much to do. I'll have to live with shorter cavalettis on the north tower, closer to the axis of the cable and askew—the worst kind.

I'll have to live is the part of my thought I retain.

I check on my crown: no new panels there, ah!

For a second, I catch myself wanting like a toddler to slap the wrist of my twin north tower, and to chastise, "Bad, bad aluminum panels!"

BOW & ARROW

My eyes have now adjusted to the absence of light. Despite the frantic work, I am glancing at the north tower every three seconds. Gradually, a minuscule antenna rises from its smooth, dark silhoutte, dead center. It's Jean-Louis's arm, now erect and motionless: he is ready to shoot and is waiting for my signal.

I am supposed to raise my arm for ten seconds in response, and then Jean-François and I are to lie flat for protection under the foot-high window-washer tracks. Jean-Louis will count to ten, aim the bow at the New Jersey shore to allow for the strong westerly wind, and shoot the arrow carrying the fishing line. As rehearsed, the arrow will land near the center of my rooftop.

I am not ready.

And we don't have a signal for "I am not ready."

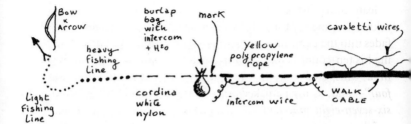

Having unrolled the walk-cable, I am still fighting with the cavaletti lines—a wrong move uncoiling them would mean an extra hour of work, time I don't have. And I am still running back frequently to the narrow staircase opening where Jean-François's head is still plunged, on the lookout.

The nonstop unrolling of so many feet of cable is taking a toll on my back, so I whisper to Jean-François to take over, and we exchange tasks. But kneeling on the cold concrete with my head upside down is unbearable; I prefer breaking my back. With a millisecond of admiration—Wow, how does he do it?—I order my friend back to his post.

Finally, the cavalettis are laid out.

Valiant Jean-Louis! For what must be twenty minutes, he keeps his arm raised for me to see. Before I signal in answer, I look at Jean-François's kneeling silhouette, which is more or less in the bull's-eye. Shall I pull him away from his watch, or risk having him shot? I snigger at the image of early workers discovering a still-warm French corpse, arrow through the heart, amid abandoned ropes and cables—how would the headlines read? But I can't finish the rigging alone!

In six silent giant steps, I reach Jean-François and swiftly tiptoe him back to the relative safety of the steel tracks.

I raise my arm.

We count to ten, then dive under the tracks, trying to leave no limbs exposed. We hide our heads in our hands, but I pry open my friend's fingers so that he can keep watch on the staircase opening, and I uncover one of my eyes to keep Jean-Louis's arm in view.

Jean-Louis brings his arm down and raises it again, in acknowledgment of my signal. Then the arm lowers slowly and fades into the penumbra of the rooftop. Jean-Louis must be starting his ten-count before shooting. Jean-François counts with me in a whispered echo—"One-*one*, two-*two*, three-*three*, four-*four*"—and, as my panicked voice falls silent, he finishes: "*Five-six-seven-eight-nine-ten!*"

Like escaping prisoners, we hold our breath and lie perfectly still: we are listening to the night, 1,350 feet above the ground.

Nothing!

Shouldn't the arrow be airborne already? Did the fishing line break?

Was that a faint metallic *cling* I just heard?

I send Jean-François back to his watch at the staircase; I go hunting for the arrow, but my legs are cottonlike; I taste bile. I am worn out, about to faint, in raging despair. Jean-Louis has missed. The coup has failed.

A physical defiance has me crawling in the dark on all fours, in all directions. Nothing! I sweep the rough concrete surface, scraping my hands. Still nothing!

Back on my feet, crouched over to hide my silhouette, I run back and forth along the north edge of the roof. Nothing, nothing! I pass again, this time scraping against the beams of the perimeter, one arm raised above my head in case the line is floating in the breeze, one arm stretched out toward the lower ledge in case the thread is caught there. Nothing. No thread. No arrow.

I am determined to find this invisible thread in the windy darkness—even to invent it! Without thinking, I tear off my clothes. My naked body will locate what my hands could not. Arms out, like a blind beggar in a Bruegel painting, forgetting to hide, I scout the obscurity, I stumble over the equipment, I fall. I collect cuts and scratches, but no fishing line.

Incensed, I attempt to calm my thoughts by leaning against the northwest corner and staring dementedly at the murky Hudson River, where the arrow may have drowned—when on my hip I feel the incredibly sweet caress of a fishing line undulating in the chilly wind.

I walk my fingers along the line until they reach the arrow, which is—unbelievably—delicately balanced on a steel channel girt over the abyss. Another half inch to the west and it would have missed the tower. I close my hand around the arrow just as a sudden draft threatens to dislodge it.

Now I am in heaven—and freezing from head to toe.

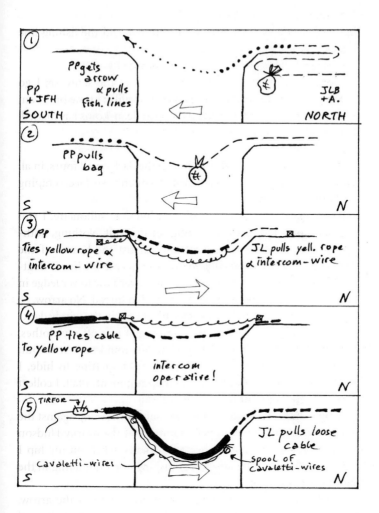

I dash to share the news with Jean-François, who—head still inverted in the stairwell—can't see I'm naked. I pull the fishing line across and get dressed. Then comes the second fishing line, heavier and stronger—I can feel Jean-Louis's hands paying it out.

Got it!

I keep pulling. It's so smooth, so easy, I laugh out loud.

Now I have the cordina, the white nylon parachute cord. I tension it a bit, fasten it to the flat bar with a clove-hitch-in-the-bight, and add a black dot with a marker, as does Jean-Louis, I'm sure. Later, we'll know who won a contest we started in Vary, to guess the distance between the two anchor points.

I wave at Jean-Louis in the obscurity, even though he probably can't see me.

I allow myself a moment of rest. Then I climb down onto the lower ledge, carefully lean over the emptiness, and pee onto the plaza, scribing the word *happiness*.

BAGFUL OF WORDS

Rigging continues effortlessly. I bring in more and more of the loose cordina until the north tower resists. I cannot see, but I know they are now attaching the burlap bag containing my intercom unit, the water, and a few tools. I wait. I get a signal. I resume pulling. I feel the weight of the precious burlap bag dangling in the air. I'm so impatient to talk to Jean-Louis, I want to be able to pull it to me in one unbroken stroke. The thin line, now loaded, hurts my fingers. The cordina stops! What's happening? I pull harder, but it's stuck.

Oh, Jean-Louis must have hit a little knot, courtesy of Murphy's Law. I wait for him to untie it.

Pulling again brings me only a few inches of cord, and those are given by the elasticity of the nylon fibers, not by Jean-Louis's hands. I wonder if the burlap bag is stuck on the north tower's crown, invisible to Jean-Louis in the dark. I pull and I pull.

Nothing!

I cast a temporary clove-hitch-in-the-bight around the flat bar and run to steal Jean-François from his watch. Dizzy from holding his head upside down for so long, his knees crushed, the poor lad must hold my arm to limp to the cordina. We pull and we pull to our strength's limit. To no avail.

I send Jean-François back to his post—he goes crawling—and I keep looking into the void, baffled: how can a line be stuck between two roofs?

Suddenly I make out the bag: it's swinging in the dark, less than sixty feet from me!

This time I have something tangible to fight for. I set my eyes on the bag and go for it with all my might. The bag dances even more, but does not get closer. I pull until my arms give up.

I remember reading somewhere that the legs are stronger than the arms, so I sit down, legs bent, feet against the edge's flat bar, holding the cordina with both hands. I try to extend my legs. I push and I push, until my calves shake. The bag does not budge. Once more I try, this time letting frustration and rage replace brute strength. The bag comes my way an inch, then refuses to move any more.

This is an enigma.

I tie the cordina, stand up calmly, and try to reason. A master of rigging, I must come up with an answer. I cannot. It hurts. So I do what I've done all my life. I rely on intuition. My silly childish intuition whispers to me the most preposterous advice: "If it does not work now, wait. Maybe it'll work later."

I wait for ten minutes, hands on hips, staring at the bag dangling in midair. Then I go for the cordina, but at the last moment change my mind: if time is solving the problem, let's give time more time! Proudly I stand, arms crossed, as I watch the bag for another ten minutes.

"That should do it," whispers the silly child in me.

I untie the cordina and pull. The bag glides towards me. I keep pulling with ease. The bag lands softly at my feet. Oh! There's a little note from Jean-Louis taped to the tie: "Welcome."

I open the bag joyfully and connect my part of the intercom to the 200-foot electric cord already laid out on my roof. To pass that cord to the north tower, I will pair it with the thick yellow polypropylene rope. I quickly tie one end of the yellow rope to my end of the cordina, using a double-sheet-bend. A few feet from the knot, I make fast one end of the cord to the yellow rope with a double-rolling-hitch with six round-turns. I signal the north tower to pull the cordina. With one hand, I ease the yellow rope into the darkness while I gently pay out the cord with the other, until it hangs under the full length of the rope. The yellow rope is light and smooth, easy on the hand, and all goes very well.

A few minutes later, the north tower is connected!

Jean-Louis awaits my greetings.

"What the hell happened?" I imagine my words walking across the chasm along the thin electric wire, all the way to my good friend's ears.

"Hey, Philippe, didn't you think that if we didn't give you the cordina, it could be we were having a problem here? Couldn't you just wait?"

"What problem?"

"Well, the bag was already two thirds across, and dancing a lot, when I saw a guard two floors beneath you, looking out the window. Because of the slack in the cord, the bag was swinging a bit above his head, but right in front of him. It was a miracle: he was looking at my tower, he was looking down at the plaza, but he never looked up. He would have seen the bag, even in the dark! So I stopped. But you kept pulling. And the more you pulled, the more the bag was dancing!

"I tried to stop your pulling, but god, you were pulling like mad. I guess when you're mad, you're pretty strong. I had to ask Albert to come help me! And then we waited a good twenty minutes. And then the guard left. So we released the cordina."

The next thing out of the burlap bag is the bottle of water. I have an excuse for not sharing with Jean-François: he is too far away, absorbed in his upside-down vigil. Just as I take a mouthful of the quenching liquid, two hands grab my neck from behind. I spurt out all of it, coughing with fright.

"You scared me," I reproach Jean-François, who has come to announce that his guard is gone. "Let's run for it," I say, closing the bottle in a hurry; another excuse for not offering a drink to my friend.

We fly down the stairs; we bring all the equipment to the roof in three trips. "The shoes!" I go to retrieve them while Jean-François starts unwrapping the balancing pole. We painstakingly assemble it and hide it. Why? I couldn't say.

I have the urge to give Jean-François a big hug, but that would be a loss of time. I run from one task to another, trying to anticipate what the next move will be, which I'm rarely able to do. When the silent night is pierced by the intercom's repeated buzz—too loud even at the lowest volume—I drop whatever I am doing and dash to answer, banging into the equipment and cutting myself on the sharp edges of beams.

This bruising routine will be repeated throughout the night.

Laboratory rats in their cages, when hit by an electric jolt, take it a few times, then learn to avoid it. Not I.

PAS DE DEUX

Did you ever play hide and seek in the woods? Choose an oak tree the size of a medieval tower, behind which you wait? When the seeker arrives at your tree and starts walking around it, you do the same. When he stops, you stop. He keeps circling, so do you.

If you stay silent, this diametrically opposed choreography can go on for a long time—unless your pal suddenly turns about and runs into you.

A guard (the same guard?) appears on our roof, preceded by the static of his walkie-talkie. Jean-François, by the tower's corner, has time to lie flat under the tracks and play dead. I am trapped near the center of the roof, with only some concrete walls and steel structures between the guard and me.

He walks around the core of the roof. So do I.

He stops. I stop.

He keeps circling. So do I.

He leaves. I stay.

One such dance is enough!

I quickly gather a few empty cans and other junk, and construct midstaircase a miniature Calder mobile no human being could avoid banging against in the dark.

I bring Jean-François over, to make him aware of the trap and to make sure he admires its cleverness as much as I do.

With peace of mind, we return to our work.

BEFORE LETTING GO

Before I let the walk-cable go into the void—that is, before I signal for Jean-Louis and Albert to pull the yellow rope to which I have tied one end of the cable—I do something Papa Rudy taught me.

I take the other end of the cable, make one half turn around a steel column, bring the two parts together, and hold them side by side with a U-clamp loosely bolted by hand. A nice touch is to leave a little wrench with the right socket nearby—if need arises, one can tighten the two nuts of the clamp. The whole thing is childish, but it reassures me that the cable will not go anywhere, as Omankowsky used to say.

Jean-Louis and Albert pull the yellow rope. Jean-François and I pay out the heavy cable. The wire crosses fluidly and disappears slowly into darkness.

Soon we all must slow down. The cable is heavier, it passes one foot at a time. Then it becomes easier, as if the steel rope is taking on a life of its own. The cable accelerates its descent. Jean-François and I try to slow it down, but its weight and speed are too great, it threatens to pull us into the void. We have to let go.

Instantly, the cable dives full-speed into the abyss, with an apocalyptic scream. I hurl my friend out of the way as deadly loops of wire jump overboard. I dash to the other end of the cable. I grab the little wrench. I tighten the U-clamp as fast as I can. Behind me, I hear the roar of 200 feet of out-of-control cable. Just as the clamp is finally tight, the last loops of cable unfold so swiftly that I dive to the side.

The shock is terrible. The column vibrates. The clamp slides. The strands under the clamp emit a little blue smoke.

Silence returns, as if nothing has happened.

On my side, due to the devil's fastest rigging job, the cable is actually in place.

On the other side, the cable now hangs in a giant U at the end of the yellow rope, which my accomplices will have to pull and pull and pull and pull.

Why the Herculean punishment?

A LESSON IN RIGGING

Horror! Night has given up on me. It has ordered dawn to unfold gradually the drapery of its lighter tones.

Anxiety tints my blood. Time is of the essence. Am I going to make it? No room in the clock for mistakes.

When I tighten the cable, any error in the rigging will mean death of the coup, death of the cable, or death of the wirewalker. To make sure I have not committed any errors, I decide to describe aloud each component of the installation, and at the same time, to pass my hand over it—yes, touch it—and check it, with my eyes calmly focused.

Because this is the most important rigging of my life, I need a master of ceremonies. I ask Jean-François to watch me, to make sure I overlook nothing. I know how silly it is to invite a nonrigger to such an exercise. But Jean-François, his face turned serious, boosts my confidence by being there, and I suspect he will sense if I make a mistake.

"Okay. The inclined column serving as anchor has its upper web tightly packed with overlapping pieces of wood and protected by thick carpet." I pass my hand to check, while explaining to Jean-François that the wood will act as a one-way spring in case the towers sway. The overtensioned cable will bite deeply into the wood fibers if the two roofs move apart. A second later, of course, as the rooftops return to their original position or move closer, the cable will go completely slack and stay that way—a deadly solution for the wirewalker, but a safe one for the installation, the buildings, and the people below. Anyway, it's the best I could come up with.

The reason for the carpet: I never have and never will hurt any edifice with my wire. I do not wish to leave even the tiniest scratch on the towers I love.

Jean-François nods attentively, and I go on.

On top of the carpet, a wire-rope sling stronger than the walk-cable is wrapped one-round-turn around the steel post. The two eyes of the sling, protected by heavy-duty thimbles, go into the big Lyra-shackle. And the pin of the shackle is marlinespike-tight. I introduce the marlinespike point into the pin's head and cannot screw it further.

What connects the shackle to the rear of the Tirfor is a Crosby weldless oval link, and the Tirfor pin has its safety latch on. The Tirfor handle is in place and has been twisted a quarter turn to lock it onto the machine's sleeve so that the person working the handle will not accidentally pull it free, lose balance, and fall. The Tirfor cable is already in place: its pointed end sticks out of the rear of the machine and meets no obstacle to prevent it from traveling further back; the other part of the cable, terminated by a thimbled eye and an oversize hook, is coming out of the Tirfor's mouth and is elongated toward the void. It shows no kinks or meat hooks—those deadly steel splinters sticking out. The heavy come-along is resting on a pad to keep it from vibrating. The hook of the Tirfor cable, with its safety latch engaged, catches the thimbled eye of the walk-cable, which is secured by seven—not five as is customary—heavy-duty cable clamps tightened to the right torque. Under the clamps' saddles and U-bolts, the 6 x 19 cable is compressed, but is not birdcaging at all—meaning that the wires in the strand aren't opening up. The walk-cable is perfectly cleaned. Of course, tension and sunshine will always squeeze out a small amount of the grease that lubricates the cable's core—unless you can afford to order a cable specially manufactured without grease. So on this side, as soon as the north tower team gets their end of the walk-cable and ties it to their anchor column, I am ready to pull.

On the cable, already invisible in the void, the two cavaletti plates are correctly positioned and bolted; I remember checking them. And from the plates, the two cavaletti wires (one long, one short) to be anchored at the north tower are dangling under the cable, and their ends, coiling a few extra feet, are tied securely near the connection of the yellow rope and the walk-cable. The two cavaletti wires on my side (one short, one long) are ready to be anchored and tightened by means of block-and-tackles that are already elongated. There is a figure-of-eight knot terminating each block's ropes for added security. The balancing pole is out of hiding and correctly assembled; the little bolts holding the sleeves are not overtight. And the rubber inner tube wrapped around its center—another safety feature from Papa Rudy, so the pole will not slip if it touches or hits the cable—is secured generously by electric tape.

"Well, I think this is it," I say to Jean-François, who's as pleased as I am. Then we go back to work on a myriad of details and adjustments.

On the north tower, the main job has hardly started. The cable lost between the two structures is harder to bring back than I thought. Jean-Louis and Albert use their arms to pull the yellow rope. Then they use their arms and legs. Then the intercom starts ringing on my roof. I give Jean-Louis instructions on how to improvise mechanical advantages.

The advance of daylight creates a cloud of anxiety, soon of veiled panic, over the entire operation.

The end of the cable is within three feet of Jean-Louis when Albert, who has not stopped arguing since the beginning, announces he is about to quit. "He believes we'll never make it," says Jean-Louis with bitterness. "By the way, he insists on talking with you."

Instantly comprehending that the north tower is paralyzed by a clash of egos, a language problem, a lack of rigging knowledge, and the growing daylight, I share with Jean-Louis my only solution: I need to come over! "Right now, I'll run down to the lobby, run across to the north tower, and run up to your roof! See you in less than an hour!"

"Philippe! Stop!" screams Jean-Louis over the void, then continues over the intercom. "You're going to get caught ten times before arriving here! But even if you do arrive, and you spend a couple hours getting the cable and anchoring it, you'll be caught here without your balancing pole, because don't try to tell me there's any chance for you to accomplish a complete back-and-forth from roof to roof without being caught! Plus you'll have no more legs anyway!"

I tell him that once I secure the cable on the north tower I can use the cable itself to get back to my tower, inching my way across with my hands and feet.

"Or else I go across right now," I say, obviously having lost touch with reality, "hand over hand along the cable, and then along the yellow rope. If the rope is strong enough to pull the cable, it's strong enough to support me . . . No, you're right, it's madness. Give me Albert!"

"Albert, listen! You're completely right. It looks like we're never going to make it before the construction workers arrive. But we've gotten so far, it's worth a try. I'm sure if you and Jean-Louis win another foot of yellow rope, you'll be able to grab the two coils of cavaletti wires: the cable will then be much lighter. And in the meantime, to make it easier for you guys, I'll find a way to release a little bit more of the cable on my side. But you know what? You're completely right, I agree with you one hundred percent. If we're still at it when it's bright daylight, it will mean it's too late, we'll never complete the rigging, and then it's wiser to give up. I'm not going to walk if the installation is unfinished, of that you can be sure!"

I hope my tone conceals the lie. I hear a vague sigh of approval on the other end of the line. A minute later, I feel the cable inching its way closer to the north tower.

While waiting, I turn my attention to an entanglement of thin wire-ropes around and below my departure corner. Most wires are merely wrapped around the sharp edges of the structure without any protection. Here and there, a few clamps are used, but they are assembled the wrong way, and they are not tight enough. A few turnbuckles not fitted with safety latches complete the scene. I lean over and see that, several floors below, this dangerous rigging holds a narrow aluminum working platform, long enough for thirty men and running almost the entire width of the facade. I am concerned for the men who may not realize they are venturing onto a virtual suicide board. So I go to work securing the mess until the next intercom call. And from now on, whenever I have a few seconds or a few minutes, I keep reinforcing the rigging for my brothers, the aerial construction workers.

"It's almost daylight!" I groan, my eyes wide with fatigue.

To hell with being nice. It's panic time, every man for himself. Forgetting I had sworn never to ask Jean-François, who has vertigo, to work on the lower ledge, I force him to join me immediately on the deadly cornice to anchor each of the two cavaletti wires to their respective tensioning block-and-tackle.

His back to the void, my friend climbs down the channel girts like a terrified snail. On the ledge area, he helps me while staying under the protection of the inclined columns, as far away as possible—that is, 35 inches!—from the 1,350-foot drop.

I bump into Jean-François, I knock him over; he is in my way.

I shove him; he is too slow.

I encircle him in a dance of frenzy, allowing him no time to understand he's toiling—against his will—between life and death.

Things are moving much too slowly: I bark orders in English, and Jean-François looks at me dumbfounded—I forget he does not understand a word of the language. I yell insults, I shout at him for not doing what I ask.

I instruct him machine-gun style—"Arrange-this-the-right-way! Take-care-of-that-thing-there! Come-here-continue-what-I-am-doing!"—without being sure exactly what I mean, and without remembering that Jean-François knows absolutely nothing about the art of rigging. When, to my astonishment, my friend dares to crawl onto the six-inch-wide window-washer indexing tube right on the edge of the abyss, I push him, pull him, jump over him, abusing him ever more loudly: "Faster! For god's sake, hurry up! Hold this! Shit, are you deaf? Not this, this!"

It is now close to full daylight.

The brightness in the sky magnifies my fury, increases my agitation, and intensifies my violence. To make it complete, the intercom crackles the worst news yet: "Listen, Philippe, since you told us you no longer care if we make an extra security loop to anchor the cable, Albert has completely given up!" says Jean-Louis in a sickened tone. "It's been half an hour that I pull and pull all by myself like a donkey, and the cable is coming only a millimeter at a time! But it's done; you have your first two cable clamps in the right place, well tightened. But let me tell you, he . . ."

I hang up and spring to the Tirfor area.

Downstairs, Annie lowers her binoculars and comments: "It's six a.m., they still haven't tightened the cable. Something is wrong!"

At 6:10, she's the first to announce, "The cable is moving! I see it going up! Philippe is tightening the cable!"

Indeed, standing on the roof's crown, one hand clutching a channel girt for dear life, the other vehemently working the Tirfor handle back and forth for precious tension, I am tuning my wire for the celestial symphony to follow . . .

"But why is he stopping every five minutes?" Annie questions aloud.

CATENARY CURVES

When timber framers start building a bridge, when magicians present a cord on stage, when kids play tug-of-war, when illegal wirewalkers rig a cable, invariably there is a moment when the line hangs freely between two points, and smiles.

The shape adopted in midair by such lines is called a catenary curve. The name comes from the eighteenth century, a time when *catenæ*, chains, were used instead of the yet-to-be-invented wire rope to link, to pull, to hold. Many engineers had a chain printed on their business cards or embroidered on their lapels. Complex equations were devised that would predict with precision the shape of a hanging chain according to its span, weight per link, tension, and the place in space of its two anchor points.

There is an infinite number of catenary curves, some—like people—more appealing than others.

Even in the midst of the hardest rigging job or the most demanding clandestine adventure, I never fail to pause and admire when tension brings my cable to what I consider to be its most seductive shape. Then I take a breath and smile back.

This morning, I can't resist stopping the action of the Tirfor handle to review the evolution of the curves as my cable slowly tightens. From the gigantic U of the loose cable an hour ago to the straight line I'm trying to obtain for a safe walk—not true, it's never a straight line—I have stopped to consider many a curve, and now I have one, stored forever in the daguerreotype of my memory.

Amid the hundred lights of dawn in the cable, in the sky, in the tower facing me, no one can name the shades that create such a celestial masterpiece.

A VISITOR

Now that the cable is at the right tension, we have to pull on the two block-and-tackles anchored by the lower ledge to tension the two cavaletti wires properly. This means we must play monkeys again.

Racing even more feverishly than before, I reach an even higher level of insanity. It's contagious: soon Jean-François is scampering again on the edge of the chasm, like a newborn mountain goat.

Suddenly, I stop in the middle of tying a highwayman's-hitch with one hand to hit Jean-François's shoulder extremely hard with the other. I am standing on the channel girts of the crown. I scream to him in a whisper (yes, I can do that), "*Freeze!* Someone just came on the roof! Switch to slow motion! We are two construction workers slowly starting the day! Come up, show him you're wearing a helmet, but don't look at him, and keep working! Keep working!"

I keep working, as slowly as I can, my eyes glued to the visitor. He is not a guard, not a policeman, not a construction worker, not a foreman. He looks like a regular guy. He stands there, on the last step of the small staircase, and looks around. He sees me. He sees Jean-François. He looks at us.

Nonchalantly, I pick up my gloves and take a rest, hands on hips—contemplating the work already accomplished—just as a real worker would do.

Damn, he's walking toward us. It's a long, long way to our corner—or am I so deranged that normal movements look like slow motion? As the man draws nearer, he sees the cable between the towers; I see him noticing the Tirfor. He stops for a moment where there is a difference of levels in the concrete slab, and observes at leisure the entire scene and—oh, no!—he turns his head and sees the balancing pole. Obviously, he has discovered everything. Now it's only a matter of . . . He is moving closer, still in slow motion to my eyes. He's going to . . . Years of dreaming and building the dream are going to be flattened by this man who is going to . . . to . . .

I revolt against such injustice. Blood floods full speed through my being, my brain jolts back to real time. Guided by a frighteningly unconscious impulse, I find myself walking toward the visitor. He keeps walking toward me. We are walking toward each other. Thirty feet. I keep walking. It is a duel. Twenty feet. I am looking him in the eyes. My chin is up. I feel strong. I am not afraid. Ten feet. I keep walking. I have fire in my eyes. I'm invincible. My dream is invincible. I see a short metal pipe on the floor; I slow down and pick it up. I'm not brandishing it, I'm just . . .

The man has stopped.

He is no longer looking at me. He is admiring the site with calm assertion, as if he needs to communicate his desire to avoid confrontation. Has he felt an intangible electricity in the air, a portent of doom?

The mysterious visitor—probably a businessman who works in the tower and wants to admire dawn before going to his desk—leaves my roof as he appeared, slowly and peacefully.

I take it there will be no duel today.

Except the one scheduled between the void and me, where it is written—I wrote it—"Both sides will survive."

"THE WHEEL! THE WHEEL!"

The sky casts off gray, tries on a pale blue cloak, wants to turn brighter still. I had better catch up with the rising sun!

It's 6:45 a.m. below. My friends—anxiously watching through shared binoculars, awaiting my first step on the wire—are oblivious to the jostling of the early commuters coming out of the subway.

Up here, time has lost all sense.

On my roof, the rigging is basically in place. Now I must fine-tune it, which means running back and forth, pulling here, loosening there, placing antivibration devices, straightening the cable, aligning the cavalettis—the most exhausting part of the operation.

Each passing second brings me closer to the ultimate disaster: the wire will not be ready on time. It simply means my life will be shorter than I had anticipated—because I am going to charge onto that goddamn cable, any which way. I'm going to throw myself onto the nightmarish tightrope of my dream.

A stubborn automaton with very little spring power left, dead-weighted with fatigue, heartsick, I drag myself back to work, toiling against the odds. I keep watching the giant metal wheel hanging above a scaffold of beams at the center of my roof—the assembly for the freight elevator that brings construction personnel to the highest floors. A minute or so after the wheel starts turning, foremen and workers will be on my roof.

I catch Jean-Louis making wide sweeping gestures.

The intercom has been buzzing me for ten minutes! Racing back and forth with Jean-François, I've forgotten to pay attention to it. Jean-Louis gives me the worst technical news: after tensioning their first cavaletti (the short one), they realized they had made a mistake—they let the little metal plate that is bolted to the walk-cable turn on itself. The two small wings of the device are facing the sky instead of the ground, creating a sharp obstacle for my sliding feet on the wire. Jean-Louis awaits my instructions.

Shielding my eyes from the daylight, I focus my gaze on the problem. The cavaletti plate will certainly impair my crossing, but it's more dangerous than that. At any moment during the walk, the plate might slide into a different position; or worse, swaying under tension, the cavaletti lines might force the plate open, sending it into the void with the cavaletti wires, and my walk-cable, suddenly freed, will jump up without warning.

Since I know it will take a good half hour to fix the problem, and since thanks to Papa Rudy's safety advice the plate is held by three bolts instead of the two I normally use, my response is to the point: "Too late! Tighten to death. I'll deal with it."

With everything we can find, Jean-François and I are building a barricade around the anchor of the cable, and we add to it a DO NOT DISTURB sign—in the foolish hope that it will prevent the first workers and the police from touching the cable.

Again I see Jean-Louis waving in distress—again I have forgotten to attend to the intercom's buzz. His latest rigging misfortune is even more dramatic to me: he's unable to tie his second cavaletti wire, the long one, to its block-and-tackle at the foot of the inclined column. Because of the location change necessitated by the encroachment of the aluminum panels, he is now dealing with many extra feet of quarter-inch wire-rope and can't use the eye with thimble I had prepared at the extremity of the line. "Plus," Jean-Louis tells me, "this time Albert has really given up. He's packed his bag. I think he's changing back into his business-man's clothes."

For me there is only one solution, a very bad solution: "Forget about it!" I tell him just to wrap the cavaletti wire directly around the foot of the column, and to finish by making a festival of knots. I'll give him some slack, and when he's done, I'll retension my two cavalettis. "It won't be great, but it might work."

I drop to the lower ledge and loosen my two cavalettis, wiping out thirty minutes of painstaking precision work in thirty seconds. Back on the upper roof, I see a sight that makes me scream in ter-ror: "The wheel! The wheel! It's turning!"

At the top of its heavy support, the gigantic steel wheel is screeching as it gathers speed.

I yell last-minute instructions to Jean-François and jump, liter-ally jump, from the upper edge to the deadly lower ledge. One of my feet misses the indexing tube; one of my legs falls over the void.

I retrieve my leg. "Faster! Faster! Faster!" I yell to Jean-Louis, who is still struggling to anchor his cavaletti.

Jean-Louis gives me a thumbs-up.

With the power of despair, I fly from one block-and-tackle to the other—I tie, I take up the slack, I tension—why does it take an eternity? To hell with fine-tuning; I fly back up and roll onto the roof like a martial artist. The elevator wheel whirls and screams. I see smoke from the motor.

My last communication with the north tower uses all the energy I have left. I concentrate on sending intelligible words across the air. I tell Jean-Louis to get dressed, so that no one can seize him as a rigging accomplice. I tell him I'll wait to start walking until he's back at the edge of his roof, movie camera in hand. "Make sure

you film the first steps before taking pictures!" is my last suppli-
cation.

Jean-Louis promises me everything. I disconnect the intercom
wire, which floats for a moment in the air currents. Good. It
reminds me the wind is about to catch up.

My dear friend quickly pulls in the free line and disappears.

"HE'S FALLING!"

To save precious time, I leap over the flat bar to the path by the
lower ledge instead of climbing down the five channel girts.
There, out of sight from my friends on the street, out of reach of
the wind, I have created a dressing room. I grab the bag with the
costume and rip it open. Frantically rummaging, I find the black
slippers and put them on, I jump into the pair of black pants. I've
already torn off my shirt, but I cannot find my black turtleneck
sweater. I pour the contents of the bag onto the concrete floor,
and madly throw item after item over my shoulder, desperately
searching for the missing piece.

A quarter mile below, my watching friends scream in unison as
Annie howls, "He's falling!"

With horror, they see a black silhouette surging from my corner of the south tower and falling into the void. At first it's a
human shape, whirling and twirling, then it turns into what my
friends conclude looks like a piece of cloth; their moment of terror passes.

What a tragedy—seconds before my entrance onto the stage of
my life, my costume is incomplete!

It is crucial; it is essential for me to appear in the sky dressed as
the street-juggler performing on the sidewalks, being arrested by
the police. It is my revenge against authority, my statement to my
street audience, my ... Heartbroken, I turn my head to the sky—
help! And I hurl down at Annie the worst invectives. No doubt,

after mending the sweater, she forgot to put it back in the bag. Little do I know that in my excitement, I have sent the garment flying!

Grumbling, I put on the thin, dark gray V-neck sweater I brought as an undergarment. It has a pocket roughly stitched in the back that holds my passport and a neatly folded twenty-dollar bill.

What a shame.

WILD CAT

Back on the upper roof, I am standing precariously on the turntable of the window-washer, about to pick up the balancing pole, when Jean-François offers me the water bottle. Ignoring my friend, I turn my back to the wire to create the sense that I am backstage and, trembling with thirst, bring the liquid to my lips but stop. I'd better wash my hands and face. In an instant, the precious liquid is gone, and my face is still dirty. I lick it with my paws like a cat. A wild cat. Jean-François spits in a rag and wipes the grease off my hair.

I turn, face the wire, and look down at the balancing pole. I dry the sweat on my palms against the sides of my pants. With joy and fear, I whisper to Jean-François, as if we were both going to step on the cable, "Let's do it. Let's go!" For him, it is the password to victory. I am not aware that he is waving his helmet in a dance of happiness. I am concentrating on bending down so my fingers can reach the pole.

THE FIRST STEP

All of a sudden, the density of the air is no longer the same. Jean-François ceases to exist. The facing tower is empty. The wheel of the elevator no longer turns.

The horizon is suspended from east to west.

New York no longer spreads its infinity. The murmur of the city dissolves into a squall whose chill and power I no longer feel.

I lift the balancing pole. I jounce it, maneuver it between my fingers to find its center, to accustom my arms to its weight, as I do before each of my performances.

I approach the edge. I step over the beam.

I place my left foot on the steel rope.

The weight of my body rests on my right leg, anchored to the flank of the building.

I still belong to the material world.

Should I ever so slightly shift the weight of my body to the left, my right leg will be unburdened, my right foot will freely meet the wire.

On one side, the mass of a mountain. A life I know.

On the other, the universe of the clouds, so full of unknown that it seems empty to us. Too much space.

Between the two, a thin line on which my being hesitates to distribute whatever strength it has left.

Around me, no thoughts. Too much space.

At my feet, a wire. Nothing else.

164

My eyes catch what rises in front of me: the top of the north tower.

60 meters of wire-rope. The path is drawn.

It's a straight line. Which rolls on itself. Which sways. Which sags. Which vibrates.

Which is ice. Which is three tons tight. Ready to explode. To dissolve. To dissolve me. To choke me. To swallow me. To throw me silently across the void jammed between the towers.

The wire waits.

The unknown, the infinite, the joyous reaper stretches out its arms and hides its face. Its arms of thousands, tens of thousands, of tons of concrete, glass, steel, and threat. A gaping mouth 110 stories deep, more than 400 meters tall.

An inner howl assails me, the wild longing to flee.

But it is too late.

The wire is ready.

My heart is so forcibly pressed against that wire, each beat echoes, echoes and casts each approaching thought into the netherworld.

Decisively, my other foot sets itself onto the cable.

MEETING THE GODS

Inundated with astonishment, with sudden and extreme fear, yes, with great joy and pride, I hold myself in balance on the high wire. With ease.

A not-yet-recognizable taste seizes my tongue—the longing to soar.

I commence my walk, but my body remains motionless.

Is this fear?

The gods in me.

Determination! Tenacity! Now is the moment. The moment is given unto your hands—hold on to this balancing pole. The moment is given unto your feet—hold on to that steel cable. Are they telling you, "Give up"?

As in a dream, with immense effort I manage to displace myself through space.
Is this courage?

The gods in the balancing pole.

Keep blowing life into those artificial arms. Bring them, bring it to life. Keep it heavy, solid. Keep it horizontal. You are no device, no instrument. You are an extension of my arms, of me. Keep breathing. Keep oscillating. You are life, my life. Say I, "Carry it! Carry my life across."

The wire detaches itself from the tower behind me. Together we undertake our aerial journey, making a hole in the sky watching us.

The gods in my feet.

They are so knowledgeable, so talented.

If they allowed the soles of the feet to land flat on the cable, they would color the walk with inelegance and danger. Instead they ask the sole—and the sole complies—to land delicately on the steel, toes first. And to slide down an alert sole, not a dormant one, so that the sole feels the cable is not a flat surface but a curve. And the sole asks its flesh to find as much of that cylindrical cable as possible, to embrace it, to hang on to it. It is a safe embrace.

The gods in my feet know how not to hit the cable, how not to make it move when each foot lands. How do they know? They worked that out during their endless days of rehearsals. They know the slightest addition to the vivacious dance of the catenary curve would mean peril for the wirewalker. They ask the feet to land on the steel rope in such a way that the impact of each step absorbs the swaying of the cable, its vertical oscillations, and its twisting along the axis of the walk; the feet answer by being gentle and understanding, by conversing with the wire-rope, by enticing the huffing and puffing living entity above them to let go of his rage to control.

Wirewalker, trust your feet!

Let them lead you; they know the way.

This is the first crossing. Wire and I together, we voluptuously penetrate the cloudy layer that melts as we approach, as we pass between the twin towers of New York City's World Trade Center. I walk on air that softens under each step. I glide each foot. I cut through the whitish lump of breeze with the knife of my balancing pole.

I walk on the wire like a funambulist.

The gods in the wire-rope.

Werner, mad movie director, we have not met at the time of this walk. You have not yet read my treatise *On the High Wire*; it's still to be published. But somehow I hear your comments on my writing, the comments you will share with me a few years from now. You salute the cable I walk on, the cable I transcend, the cable I celebrate. You say: "Be respectful. Be gentle. His soul is soft. Do not hurt him." You tell of wire-ropes aching with tension,

about to break. You say, "Their inner threads glow red in anger." And you know what you are talking about, because you pulled a ship over a mountain.

My eyes weld to the metal of the arrival column, still far away, yet coming toward me. I approach the dreaded middle of the crossing, where gravity is at its most barbaric, exposure at its fiercest. Terror tints my blood.

Space no longer contains itself. The sky swallows me. What a handsome death! What a glorious delirium, to steal in that way the secrets of weightlessness!

The cable feigns he does not know me.

My arms that hold the long pole . . . The soles of my feet that press the morning vapor . . . The cable that absorbs the dew . . . I pass the middle point.

Am I going to remember? To whom could I relate? Did I see? Or was it only air? Does one escape victorious from a dream forged at such height?

The gods of the void, of space: are howling. Chanting. Screaming. All at once and in unison! I hear you.

The wind passes behind me. I allow myself one breath. One pause. I let my face harbor a smile, the way humans do.

I nail the cable down. I force him to tremble no longer. I abandon him there and walk away a few steps, supported by the atmosphere agglutinating against the huge wall I'm approaching.

The second cavaletti being a stride away, I feel safe to perform my kneeling salute: the balancing pole rests on the right thigh as the right hand takes off in a fluttering of fingers, something pure.

Among the crowd 1,350 feet below, someone shouts, "He's saluting! He's saluting!" It's Annie.

The gods in my friends who are watching from the street. Below, so far below. Each has his or her own. Each kneels, prays. Do gods pray? "Be careful! Of course you are! Fragile Philippe, you look so fragile, so strong!" Each with hands up to support me, to implore my success. Each with hands down to receive me if I fail.

But for the crowd, what I just did will remain invisible.

Barely will it distinguish a human being up there, strolling upon a thread . . .

I rise to my feet, beg the wire not to betray me, beg the cavaletti plate not to break open as I carefully step over it, and continue the crossing, finally free, finally alone.

The gods of the towers. Breathing, swaying . . . Let me go. Let me pass. Let me arrive, let me reach you.

Time regains its course as I accost the skyscraper that has allowed itself to be conquered. The wind rises, indecisive. Is a hurricane in the making? The distant murmur of an awakening city succeeds in distracting me from the silence I was listening to on the high wire. I set the balancing pole safely aside.

The otherworldly colors of the sky rainbow back to a familiar background.

I can see Jean-François dancing with joy on the south tower.

Jean-Louis is looking at me through the lens of his camera. His accomplice—the American—rushes to me and gives me a strong embrace; he urges me to catch my breath.

The gods in my friends who are standing on the rooftops. Jean-Louis, from the beginning of this adventure you have been generous, driven, and superbly faithful to the cause; by your relentless intransigence you have saved the coup more than once. Jean-François, you smiled and laughed your way into the artistic crime of the century! You know nothing about the wire, nothing about skyscrapers, nothing about New York City—you don't even speak a word of English besides *yes*. *Yes*, you jumped in without hesitation to improvise your responsibility in the coup. *Yes*, you will keep protecting me until it's over. And *yes*, you do not care about the consequences.

And you, the unenthusiastic you—I'll hear about it by the end of the day—you who slowed and almost halted Jean-Louis's race to the roof. You who refused to help him pull the cable, who exhorted him to give up. You who gave up! You who despite your promise brought cameras to the scene, betraying Jean-Louis, betraying me. Without you, false friend, I would not be on that wire. I thank you, all half of you.

I disengage myself from the embarrassing hug to go inspect the cable's anchor point. Everything is fine. Next I climb down the crown, very carefully, to straighten the cavaletti's attachments.

As I move along the ledge, retightening one cavaletti after the other, I can't resist the visual dive: I glide in, feel the width of the abyss, I slide down and taste its depth, with delight I brush by the

marble plaza at street level, then I hurtle back up along the silver facades onto the dazzling surprise of my sight landing exactly where it started.

I climb back onto the roof.

Peacefully stretched across the vertiginous absence of terrain, my wire-rope magnetically demands me.

I sit down on the wire, balancing pole on my lap.

Leaning against the steel corner, I offer to myself, for a throne, the highest tower ever built by man; for a ceremonial carpet, the most savagely gigantic city of the Americas; for my dominion, a tray of seas wetting my forehead; while the folds of my wind-sculpted cape surround me with majestically mortal whirls.

I rise, standing up on the wire.

The gods of all three, of all five, of all dimensions. Of time.

You have presented me with an otherworldly offering. I am no longer blind, I am letting myself laugh. There—line evaporating from the maritime crest, line holding up the whiter shade of the pale sky with a fleeting trace of dark blue, line of horizon: you finally appear to me, in curved perfection, while at your side navigate three merchant ships of distant provenance and one suspension bridge.

You have graced me with a new set of ears and eyes: I can hear what my spectators in the streets shout and whisper . . . I can see the traffic made of automobiles with passengers, made of ants scurrying about. Under my influence, the ants are no longer able to escape, they slow to a halt, they look at me as in submission.

You have heightened my senses. You have empowered me.

I am grateful.

A siren's howling puts an end to my daydreaming.
Kicking with my heel, I wake up the cable.
With a whip of the head, I start walking.
And walking, and walking.

178

The gods of departure, the gods of arrival. Gods of all voyages be praised. The day of today witnesses a sacred expedition. A cyclic path. The repetitive bliss of exploration, the same, never the same. A crossing. The pilgrimage of a mortal and a mortal pilgrimage. A mythological journey.

I promenade from one end of the cable to the other, back and forth.

I stare proudly at the unfathomable canyon, my empire.

My destiny no longer has me conquering the highest towers in the world, but rather the void they protect.

This cannot be measured.

And you, gods of the billion constellations. Today I will not greet you. Unless I remain on the wire all morning, all day, all afternoon, until evening, until dusk, until night. I want to. I will not.

Do not provoke an eclipse, do not show up, do not shine!

But watch closely.

You're not going to believe your zillion eyes.

Victorious, I linger at the very middle of the crossing, exactly where the void, now defeated, used to vent its might.

I even sit down and survey the scene.

I rejoice at witnessing the disorder created by the announcement of my aerial escapade. The anthill is in turmoil! Voices and sirens scream orders and counterorders on the roofs and in the streets, but I hear mostly the streets, where the voice of the crowd overcomes that of emergency units.

The gods in the crowd. Simpleton gods. A crowd of gods interrupting one another: *Jump! Fall! Don't fall! He's mad! What for? Bravo! My god!* (Do gods believe in God?)

You are noisy and vain. Yet you keep all those pairs of eyes riveted to the sky, you hold all those mouths open in awe, or closed in fear, or letting go of each person's clamor. You! How right, how human of you! And you keep adding more souls to the multitude: there were hundreds, then thousands. I will be told they ended up at a hundred thousand.

You keep shifting their hearts from fear to happiness. When I leave the wire, they will shout "Bravo!" to me, in awe and laughter. I call "Bravo!" to you.

From that sitting position, the time of a wish—a dash of arrogance?—I lean back smoothly into a superb lengthening. I am now lying down.

The gods in the air below. Almighty void, we conversed earlier, at the time of my first visit, when we first met. You did not reveal yourself then, as you do this morning. Magnificent you are! And yes, oh, how terrifying! You terrify others, not me. Not today. No.

The gods in the air above. Hovering down, closer to me, metamorphosing into seabirds. I know who you are.

With a matadorlike gesture, one hand lets go of the balancing pole, twirls past my shoulder, and influences the other arm, seemingly in abandon, to wave in the monumental breeze.

I dedicate my shiny steel path, quivering with sun, to the oceans wetting the horizon, to that bird passing far above, to everything and everyone remaining distant from the ground, and I breathe like never before. Such outlaw felicity, I confess, brings me to sleep. I'm falling asleep.

The roof of the south tower is invaded by the police.

Jean-François is arrested.

On the north rooftop, Albert, who has not stopped taking pictures, runs away. Jean-Louis snaps his last shot and clears out. Below the roof, he barely has time to dive into a pile of cardboard boxes as fifteen policemen surge from the staircase, rushing to the roof.

At a speed of seventy kilometers an hour, the emergency elevator brought them to the 107th floor within eighteen seconds. The officer in charge follows orders: he must report each phase of "Operation Help/Suicide," to security headquarters. Within seconds, the Port Authority of New York and New Jersey, owner of the towers, announces, "Reinforcements on the way!"

At the same instant, at the point of Manhattan, the Aerial Guard Helicopter puts its blades into motion. Forty seconds later, it circles the crime scene at regulation altitude.

Already, a news bulletin is reporting the event on all the radio stations. Television networks are sending their crews downtown.

Ambulances, rescue vehicles, fire trucks, and police cars—with furious alarms—are forcing their way through the clogged traffic.

Subway trains continue to discharge their human swarm, which clumps together at the foot of the towers. Everyone tries to make out the tiny spot in the sky everyone is talking about. Taxi drivers abandon their cabs in the middle of the street to run and see.

Morning traffic is paralyzed.

Wall Street stops counting and looks up.

On my roof a man in uniform, probably the chief, demolishes the barricade we built, approaches the area where the cable is linked with the tensioning device, bends over the void, and observes me.

That's when I decide to wake up.

A dry air current caresses my nape.

I straighten up and again sit on the wire.

The gods of the wind. Pulsating.

It's mostly you, Aeolus. We've met before. Call to me, but whisper!

One word at a time. Speak slowly, speak softly.

Do not, do not, stand up, do not ruffle your chiton, do not take your sandals off, do not undress in preparation for putting on celebratory garments—do not.

Do not move. Be quiet. I beg you.

A caravan of clouds is hard on the heels of the sky. Heaven modifies its appearance. Rain comes.

The city has changed face. Its maddening daily rush has transformed into a magnificent motionlessness. It listens. It watches. It ponders.

My heart is so light I dare to look down, repeatedly.
    I align my sight with the sheer wall face falling from my wire.
    A vertical of such perfection.
    I don't believe my feet!
    One thousand three hundred and fifty feet of free fall—a hundred meters higher than the Eiffel Tower!

So, you,
    the gods in me,
    the gods in the balancing pole,
    the gods in my feet,
    the gods in the wire-rope,
    the gods of the void,
    the gods in my friends who are watching from the street,
    the gods of the towers,
    the gods in my friends who are standing on the rooftops,
    the gods of all dimensions,
    the gods of departure, the gods of arrival,
    and you,
    gods of a billion constellations,
    gods in the crowd,
    gods in the air below, gods in the air above,
    gods of the wind . . .
    Why is it, this morning, the first time you gather?
    Why don't you congregate more often?
    Will there be a next time?

To receive the answer, I lean back and lie down again, I stare straight into the sky.

Who is this large whitish bird silently hovering above me?
  Is it a tern? A gull? An albatross?
  Why is he staying so far above? Whom is he calling?

Are you afraid of me because my atrophied wings are featherless,
my beak fleshy, my claws unshapely?

Ah, you're lowering yourself closer: are you being curious or
readying for battle? What? Am I invading your territory? How
dare you? I fought to occupy that space, it's mine—did you fight
for it? Did your brothers and sisters? Your ancestors, maybe?
  But don't these towers reek of man, and isn't man the enemy?

Do you always look so cruel? Are you on a Promethean mission,
about to dive and cut my belly open, to tear out my liver?

How can you remain so still and yet waltz with air currents, while
I, on my thin steel strand, must adjust my balance faster than I
think, more frequently than I breathe?
  Where do you come from? The coast, a ten-minute flight? An
islet lost in the fog, not even on the map, three nights away?
Where do you rest? Inside the Statue of Liberty's torch, atop one
of the Verrazano Bridge's pillars?
  I can't smell you—can you smell me?
  Since your earlier shrieks when you discovered me, I can't hear
you: are you now voiceless? Can you hear me? Are you listening to
the faint melody I'm humming?
  Can you read the minds of other birds? Then do you know
my terrible secret: I have disguised myself as a bird *but cannot
fly?*

May we get closer?
  I will stay lying down on my wire, I will keep one arm raised
toward you, I will keep fluttering my fingers in your direction,

softly, as an invitation for you to approach, I will keep staring at you . . . Will you draw closer, softly?

Shouldn't we get acquainted?

Wouldn't it be marvelous, by the grace of Aeolus, to be granted an otherworldly friend?

I have so, so many questions—do you have any? What are they?

Wait! Are you gliding away? Why now? Why so fast?

Up, up, you are disappearing! Are the clouds angry? Are you coming back with thirty cousins to chase me away?

Please don't. I'll go soon.

FAREWELL

Shifting from the lying position to the sitting position, I notice a huge airplane passing above me, replacing for an instant the departed bird.

It seems someone is calling to me . . . in English.

Standing up again, I recognize I am at the top of the world, with all of New York City at my feet! How not to laugh with joy? I laugh with joy—and conclude the crossing with ecstasy instead of oxygen in my lungs.

As I approach the edge of the building, a bunch of arms reach out to assist me in taking the last step.

Hey! I don't need help! I haven't finished my show!

I come about. Behind me, the arms pull back. I rendezvous with the long wire and perform the "torero walk," gliding my feet, holding the pole away from my body, head high.

Near the end of the crossing, another voracious group of arms tries to grab me. An octopus! Smiling at the monster, I stop short of its reach and make another U-turn.

Next crossing—I'm absolutely no longer afraid of the wire, it is getting shorter as I stroll back and forth. Next crossing, I present the "promenade," balancing the pole on my shoulder like a pitchfork, one arm dangling, as if returning to the farmhouse after a long day's work in the field.

Someone is calling me . . .

Each new crossing begets a new walk, punctuated by fragile equilibriums, by genuflections, by salutes. Again, I sit down; again, I lie down.

Walking or motionless, I bathe in the sea waves, now on fire. Once more, this time under a ray of sun, I sit down in the middle of the cable to observe the world below.

By chance, and for the first time, my eyes focus on the octopus at the end of the wire. As I contemplate it fearlessly, it gesticulates and yells at my audacity. It is made of several uniformed men. Those men are angry.

How do you stop a wirewalker?

Suddenly the shouting hurled at me reaches my ears, because this time, the words are in French. It is Jean-François, terrified by the threats of the police—they say they're going to loosen the tension on the wire, they say they're going to send a helicopter to snatch me from mid-air—who has agreed to translate their latest message: "Stop right now or we'll take you out!"

For a second I despise Jean-François, but then I understand: he believes them.

Fascinated by a sudden wave of silence, I retreat into an endless balance on one leg, searching for the immobility that no wirewalker can ever find on a wire. Today, maybe, with the help of such prodigious height, I . . .

But I have trespassed long enough into these forbidden regions; the gods might lose patience. I offer my farewell to the New York sky: by running on the wire that shakes with allegresse, thus bringing down the curtain on the most splendid performance ever offered by a street-juggler/vagabond/high wire artist.

"Look! He's dancing, he's running!" scream my friends below, applauding my exit. They argue over the number of crossings: "He crossed six times!" "No, eight!" "He was on the wire for forty-five minutes!" "No, an hour!"

I, a bird gliding back and forth between the canyon's rims, did not count the voyages, nor did I care to record the passing of time.

THE OCTOPUS

I land where I started, on the roof of the south tower.

The octopus grabs me violently. The unforgiving concrete hurts my naked feet through the thin buffalo-skin soles of my slippers.

My wrists are forced behind my back and clamped together by much-too-tight handcuffs. I am being read my Miranda rights.

"What?"

Not understanding a word of it, I force the arresting officer to repeat the formula several times, which helps me catch my breath and think ahead. New York policemen, Port Authority representatives, World Trade Center security personnel, emergency agents, and consultants from diverse agencies surround me so tightly I cannot move. They bark at me as they would at a stinky vagrant mutt. All the while, I am fighting for breathing space and for the right to be heard: "Listen! Listen!"

"That's it, let's go! You'll speak at the precinct, we've waited long enough!" So many pairs of arms, pushing and pulling, have no problem leading me harshly to the tiny stairwell.

I resist, I shout: "No! There's going to be an accident, let me talk!"

Not in the mood to be told what to do, my arresting entourage pushes me more brutally away from the wire.

I scream, "Five seconds! Let me talk for five seconds! About the cable . . . Something terribly dangerous can happen with the rigging!"

My escort remains deaf. Force is the only reason it knows, and it intends to use plenty of it to take me away.

Out of nowhere, a tall construction worker wearing a yellow helmet cuts through the circle of my captors. He demands with authority to hear what I have to say. Raising his voice, he argues with the police before turning to me as the group falls silent: "Quick, explain yourself!"

"Well, it's imperative I loosen the tension on the cable. Right now, there's three-point-four tons, but if the towers sway, the tension will reach a terrible load and my cable will break . . . "

"Hell, if you think we give a shit about your fucking cable, we're gonna cut it with shears, that's what we're gonna do!" clarions someone who knows nothing about rigging.

"I don't give a shit about the cable," I retort, attempting to persuade the imbecile, "but if you cut a wire-rope under tension, or if it breaks by overloading, you'll get a giant whiplash: some of us on this roof will be cut in half, and the explosion will hurl large pieces of steel into the void, defacing the building and killing quite a few people in the streets." I pause and roar as dramatically as I can, "I'm warning you!" Then I point to everyone around in turn: "And y*ou, you, you, you,* and *you* are my witnesses!"

I'm being dragged to the tensioning device.

But I can't find the long handle. I remember setting it on a beam somewhere . . . No, I must have hidden it. Where?

Turmoil!

I'm tightly surrounded once more. The arresting group, vociferous again, claims my plea to release the tension is an invention, an excuse to try to get back on the wire and escape! I wish.

Again, I'm pulled away, carried away . . .

"Wait! I remember! I hid the handle inside that pipe there, so no one would alter the tension during the walk."

The come-along is fitted with its handle, and within minutes the wire is deprived of its precious inner tension. Soon it hangs loose and pitiful. It is so sad, the sky is about to weep.

As I'm being propelled to the stairwell, it starts to rain.

The most perilous episode of the six-and-a-half-year adventure—walk included—remains what follows:

Savagely, I am being pushed down the steep, narrow staircase. Exhausted from the performance, hands cuffed behind my back, I am unable to control my balance; I can't slow my descent. Gathering speed, I hurl headfirst down the stairwell where it makes an abrupt left turn. I see my skull being shattered against the concrete wall. I try to steer my body away, but the inertia is too massive, my legs too weak.

With an inch before impact, a survival instinct restores electricity to my disconnected nerves. In a flash, I bounce back from the wall before touching it and scream my rage: "Hey! Careful!"

I try to scrape against the walls to slow the rate of my descent, but twice my barbaric captors shove me forward. Twice, yelling, I succeed in avoiding collisions with concrete.

Too tired to think straight, I am convinced the intention of my escort is to kill me.

Eyes wide open with fury, body covered with goosebumps, I concentrate on escaping the death sentence—a much greater challenge than walking between the towers.

Behind me I hear, "Is he resisting arrest?"

No, only death.

REACTIONARY MEASURES

On our way to the elevator, we pass construction workers who erupt in applause and cheers when they see me. My entourage is not happy.

UNDERGROUND

I'm delighted to be pushed into the mysterious police station under the towers; I have always wanted to see what it looks like inside. Plenty of television monitors, plenty of buttons, plenty of cops shouting orders and counterorders about me. I do not try to understand what is being said to me. I let my fingers be rolled in black ink and pressed onto an arrest sheet, knowing it's a mistake; when you arrest a wirewalker, you should print his toes! No one notices that I cross my eyes as my mug shot is taken. Jean-François gets the same treatment.

In the back, I see Albert arguing with an officer. Is he being arrested? Showing his cameras, he points at the ceiling and waves some I.D., obviously playing a journalist who's been stopped on his way to the roof. Clever. They let him go, and he passes by me without showing that he knows me.

By the loading dock, my captors hurriedly squeeze me through a cluster of microphones and television cameras. My head still in the sky, I do not hear the questions but give my name and repeat, "*Immense happiness!*"

MADHOUSE

Why an ambulance, why blasting sirens, why a police motorcade? We arrive at the Beekman-Downtown hospital. Forced to lie face-down on a stretcher, I am rolled to a room labeled PSYCHIATRIC EXAMINATION. Jean-François is handcuffed to a radiator in the waiting room.

A young Pakistani doctor inspects the whites of my eyes and takes my pulse, counting in his native language.

Lying on my belly, handcuffed in the back, I keep asking, I keep begging, for something to drink.

The shrink enters. He's old, paternalistic, soft-spoken, and—I think—blinking far too many times a minute for a well-balanced human being. His head to mine, he whispers in the most articulate manner, "When—did—you—last—drink—water?"

"Are you mad?" I answer, raising my chin. "Do you know what I just did? I just spent months putting a wire without permission between the highest towers, I just astonished the world by dancing on that wire, right now the entire universe is talking about me, TV cameras are waiting downstairs. And all you want to know is the last time I drank? You're completely insane!"

The man swivels on his stool, grabs his clipboard, and jots, "The subject seems perfectly normal, although exhausted and dehydrated."

A busty young nurse comes in with a paper thimble filled with half an inch of water. She leans over my handcuffed body; my eyelids almost caress her breasts when she brings the cup to my lips. "More!" I beg. She returns with a tray filled with more paper thimbles and helps me with the same naive generosity.

"That's enough, let's go!" my police escort interrupts after I swallow the contents of three mini-cups. Too late! My tongue lubricated by the water, I manage to drop a few elated remarks to the many journalists trying to interview me.

Now we have to run a gauntlet of reporters as we enter a building flanked by stables and labeled FIRST PRECINCT. I inhale the satisfying odor of horse manure. Maybe I can jump on a steed and gallop away to freedom. My captors are not ready to release a folk hero yet; they are still busy prosecuting a criminal.

They ask me the same questions they've already asked, they inscribe the same answers on the same forms, and again they put ink on my fingers and blind me with the flash of their cameras. Through the open windows, I hear the crowd of journalists shouting to be let in, demanding to talk to me.

Chained to an armchair, I entertain myself by counting the orders and counterorders until my tough arresting escort disappears and leaves me in the hands of a group of admiring police officers. I notice a paper clip under my chair; I pick it up discreetly while scratching my ankle.

"WHY?"

Finally, the press, now a mob, is invited into a waiting room; the police leave the door ajar. I see photo lenses sticking in; I hear the motor of a television camera spying on me. Using the purloined paper clip, I pick the lock of my handcuffs. With my free hands, I borrow by surprise the officer's cap and balance it on my nose. Behind the door, the journalists scream in delight; even the officer applauds. By the time he senses something is wrong, I have recuffed my wrists!

Police officers ask for autographs. They open the door wide: I'm being fed to the press.

I talk. I talk to no end, barely listening to the questions. "How old are you? How heavy is the balancing pole? Were you scared? Was it windy up there? How did you pass the cable across? So you did it for the publicity, eh?" When I announce that Jean-Louis is the exclusive photographer of the walks and has shot 16mm footage, each press member notes his name and number.

The officer allows one last question before he puts an end to my press conference. "Why did you do it?" the reporters chorus. I

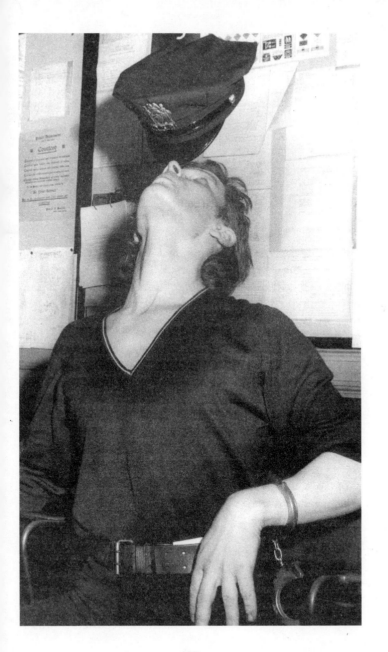

197

answer without thinking, "When I see three oranges, I juggle; when I see two towers, I walk!"

NO PROOF

Just before I'm taken away, a policeman tells me my sister is on the phone—it's Annie's clever way of getting through to me. I expect tender words of congratulations, but instead I get a matter-of-fact monologue delivered in an insulting tone: "Listen. Stop giving everyone our phone number, saying Jean-Louis has a film. He has no film. And about the photographs, I don't know if you aware of it, but Albert took pictures too, and he sold them. Jean-Louis managed to sell his, but the whole thing is a disaster. He'll tell you. He's furious. We're all furious! See you. Bye."

It is a disaster. I wanted to pass and repass in front of my eyes what went through reality so fast: the instants of the first steps, that most incredible moment of my life . . . No film almost means to me no proof. I curse Jean-Louis, the authorities holding me, the press harassing me with stupid questions. I close my eyes and get back on the wire. There, at least, I'll be out of reach! I don't notice that new captors have come to get Jean-François and me. I don't hear the new convoy's screeching tires and blasting sirens, and I certainly don't care when the thick bulletproof portal of the New York jail called the Tombs slams behind me.

THE RIGHT KEY

I am pushed into a huge, dark cage crammed with about fifty men, seated on the floor and standing. They have the same dark-toned skin, their faces are etched by the same fear, the same rancor, the same violence, and their bodies—barely covered because of the intense heat—often show the same wounds. In a corner, an unsheltered hole in the floor is the toilet. The cell stinks. It is thick with smoke. Most bulbs are broken.

I'm the only white prisoner—almost. My good friend Jean-François is still by my side. I had forgotten him!

We do not have to talk to know we both feel fear.

I take my sweater off and, putting it over my head like some of the other prisoners, fake sleeping, leaning my bare back against the door. Jean-François lights a cigarette and tries to make friends by distributing the rest around—or does his entourage come to steal them one by one? Behind me, a guard approaches, rattles his keys, opens the door, throws a new prisoner in, and slams the gate shut. I scream in pain.

I shout, "Open! Open!" not knowing how to say my skin is caught in the hinge of the gate. The guard moves away for a second, unsure whether I'm faking it. I scream and holler until he returns to the door, but he takes his time choosing the right key from his collection. He opens the door for a fraction of a second; I roll out of the steel trap and try to explore the long wound with my fingers. *What's all the noise, there's no blood!* is written on the faces of the people around me. To look like everyone else and to diffuse the pain, I force myself to smoke my first cigarette ever, but the pain is growing. I return to faking sleep, observing through my fingers the continual trade going on through the metal bars. A guard, a maintenance man, a kitchen employee, in exchange for money or cigarettes, keep passing food, drugs, messages inside the cage.

Two hours later, Jean-François and I are called to the door.

THE CONTORTIONIST, THE DISTRICT ATTORNEY,
THE THREE WHORES

Our new cage is minuscule and occupied by a skinny, wild-faced boy from Borneo. He asks if I am the man who walked between the towers—how did the news infiltrate such a dungeon?—and begs me to hire him the next time I perform. He claims to be a contortionist, and laboriously hooks one foot behind his neck for me to appreciate.

A well-dressed man frames his face between the bars of our cell, introduces himself as District Attorney Richard H. Kuh, and announces I am going to be arraigned. He proposes to drop the charges (criminal trespass, disorderly conduct, endangering my life and that of others, working without a permit, disregarding police orders—a litany of misdemeanors) in exchange for a small display of my artistry to the children of New York in a city park A few minutes of me juggling three balls under a tree in front of six kids—as long as it's on television—is all the politician desires

Not understanding the subtleties of the laws, nor the powerful man's motive, I ask if the deal has direct political implications. The D.A. assures me it does not, and we shake hands.

An hour later, Jean-François and I are taken from the Tombs and led through a maze of narrow underground passages to the courthouse. The D.A. stands by us in the courtroom. I'm given a front-row seat! Facing me, on a wooden shelf, a man of justice bored with life mumbles some gibberish to three young ladies with brown skin. Three prostitutes, one seductive and pretty, stretch their crying faces toward their accuser as if to bite him. In conclusion, the judge flutters his fingers in a gesture of disgusted ennui before he pounds the gavel. The three young women are brutally taken away to their new prison. I close my eyes.

It's our turn. The judge wakes up. Sentence is given, all charges are dropped. The assembly applauds. The cops retrieve their hardware. Jean-François and I rub our wrists and smile at each other.

SEX

As I walk down the aisle to freedom, a beautiful young girl waves at me from the bleachers. I do not know her, but I recognize her from my street-juggling crowd. I smile in return.

The steps of the courthouse are filled with reporters and journalists who scream when they see me. The questions are the same as before, but this time I listen and answer. I do not appreciate the phrasing of most of the questions and make a point of correcting it as I answer: "*No, I am not a daredevil*, I am a writer in the sky!" "*No, don't connect this with looking for a job*—I do not need anything!" All I wish to describe is the beauty of seeing from such heights the city waking up, and my elation at reaching the clouds and surprising the sky.

Through the commotion of mikes and cameras, again I see my pretty spectator smiling at me. She is waving for me to join her.

Her name is Jackie. Piercing blue eyes, boyish brown hair, adolescent demeanor—she looks wild and gentle at the same time. On the radio, she followed the events since my last crossing and learned where I was to be judged. She wanted to be "*the first citizen to personally congratulate me.*" And she does, by planting on my lips a sensuous kiss of many flavors: the flavor of freedom, the flavor of victory, of admiration, of tenderness. She rests her hand on my neck and proposes to accompany me "*wherever is my destination.*"

I discourage the press from asking more questions. I collect journalists' business cards for interviews to be scheduled later, and I look for Jean-François who, once again, I had forgotten. Delighted with the success of my first open press conference, he is sitting on the steps, patiently waiting for me to take him home.

Home! My friends must be in a frenzy waiting for our return.

Jean-François does not know the town or speak the language. Nevertheless, I order him to rush home and to tell everyone I have gone somewhere to give one last interview. Just before I disappear with Jackie, I look back and see the judge pushing aside my friend and stealing his cab.

My next interview does not happen in front of microphones and lenses, but under a silky comforter on a waterbed. It is revenge and abandon, an immense joy, the warmest entanglement, an ephemeral delirium of the senses. After all I have been through in the sky, all I have been through under the ground, after all the questions, exhausted, elated, I need, I deserve, I want the first step in my new life to be splashed with decadence, an explosion of passions.

I arrive late to the evening radio interview I had agreed to give.

It goes so well that the producer sends me home in a limousine and encourages me to keep it all night.

"First, let's rush to Chelsea!"

NORTH SIDE STORY

A television crew is waiting for me inside the apartment! Jean-Louis and Annie have tried unsuccessfully to throw them out. I'm about to succeed, in exchange for a very brief interview, when Jean-François, naked and dripping from the shower, comes into the living room looking for a towel. He is unfazed by the TV crew bribing him for comment. Three hundred dollars richer, we are finally left to ourselves. We jump into one another's arms and scream at seeing me on TV: the story is leading all of the network news broadcasts. Jim Moore bursts in with a big surprise. He spreads on the carpet the newspapers he's been collecting all day. I am on the front page of them all, in Jean-Louis's pictures—but here and there other photos show up.

Celebration is short: Jean-Louis and Annie are angry. I'm hungry.
   I win.
   I force my friends into their first limousine ride. For a moment we playfully try everything: lowering and raising the partition and windows, tasting the whiskey, zapping the tiny television screen for more views of "the Frenchman's walk." But my mood turns somber. It is late and my favorite restaurants are closing.
   We end up in a noisy joint with sawdust on the floor, coerced into ordering from a sandwich menu. JP and Barry arrive, eager to celebrate. I force the assembly to hear my long version of the south tower ordeal. But the best part of the meal comes when I finally learn what happened in Jean-Louis's north tower.
   "Well," begins Jean-Louis, taking his time eating and keeping us in suspense, "at first, it all went according to plan—you know, the plan. But then ... "

I learn that as soon as they reached the hiding place, Albert decided to change the plan: he wanted to wait for night instead of climbing to the 110th floor at 6:30 p.m. as agreed. Fortunately, Barry was still there and could translate Jean-Louis's points using rudimentary French. But alone in hiding, Jean-Louis and Albert continued to fight. Because their whispering seemed so loud, they ended up scribbling their argument on a paper towel, but the language problem made communication difficult. Jean-Louis chose to stop quarrelling and wait for the right time to come out and start climbing, no matter what, knowing that Albert would be forced to follow.

"And that's exactly what I did," continues Jean-Louis, recalling how they ran up the stairs to the 110th floor, and how they dove behind a wall of cardboard when they heard a guard approaching.

From then on, Jean-Louis's north side story is similar to mine, except they're not hanging on a beam over a void, they are crouching for hours, not changing position because of the noise it would generate. And high above their heads, an enormous wooden beam sits in fragile equilibrium, threatening to fall on them as drafts of wind make it sway. Like Jean-François and me, they can't tell if the guard is still there or has left; at times they hear him methodically checking the floor. Like us, when it's dark and everything is quiet, they come out and head for the roof. Like us, they hear voices above and hurry back to their refuge.

When all is quiet again, they argue about who should volunteer to scout the roof. Jean-Louis wants Albert to play a tourist hoping to take night shots of the city. If Albert is caught, Jean-Louis can shoot the arrow and try to rig alone. Albert finally agrees and takes a camera out of his shoulder bag. "From the beginning, I knew he had cameras with him," sighs Jean-Louis. "But what could I do, abort the coup because of that?" My friend explains how Albert returned from the roof without having seen anyone, how they tried several times to go up to the roof and how each time, always at the last moment, they had to retreat in terror, hearing voices right above them.

I interrupt Jean-Louis to explain that it was the party on our roof.

"The most fantastic moment for me," says Jean-Louis, "was when I saw you raise your hand to answer my shooting signal. I knew the coup was ninety-five percent done. And when I saw the arrow hitting the side of the building—yes, I saw it—it became ninety-eight percent!"

"And after, at the moment of the first crossing?" I ask. "What did you think?"

"Oh, I was dead, empty, and mad as hell about Albert almost ruining everything by refusing to help! And I knew you too were completely dead. You should have heard your voice over the intercom! I could see how loose the cable was, how badly guy-lined, and I thought, he's not going to be able to get across, it's insane! During the first steps, I was shivering. After pulling kilometers of lines, my fingers were simply not obeying me! My arms were absolutely dead! I was unable to control the focus of the first pictures! I was trembling with exhaustion and with, you know . . . It was frightening to see you venture onto such an untuned installation!"

It turned out there was no live footage because Jean-Louis never had the time he had been counting on to check and test the movie camera. Instead of risking it, he decided to ensure the reportage by first taking a few pictures. By the time I was lying down in the second crossing, he was ready to get the movie camera. But when he saw the cops invading my roof, he knew more would be coming for him within seconds. He barely had time to hide and, after the cops had passed, to escape.

Once on the street, he ran to the phone booths to meet everyone but, his tongue painfully pasted to his mouth by exhaustion, fright, and lack of water, he couldn't tell his story. Jim Moore dragged him to the nearest bar and ordered him eight large orange juices, which, to the amazement of the barman, Jean-Louis drank without stopping.

"Now look!" I tease Jean-Louis. "If this is the arrow"—I pick up my fork—"and this is my roof"—I clear my side of the table—

"this is where I found it!" I place the fork on the very edge of the table, ready to be dislodged by the softest vibration. "Well, that's exactly where I was aiming. I knew the arrow would be safe there!" replies Jean-Louis, laughing. Joy resurfaces as we all trade bits and pieces of an amazing story, interrupting one another loudly across a table full of empty glasses. Barry tells how he stayed glued to his desk all afternoon to monitor the telephone, except when he ran to the bathroom. But in those few minutes, his secretary informed him, there was a call—an unintelligible voice and no message. Barry bit his nails, fearful of an emergency concerning the coup, until Annie appeared as planned and life went on. Jim mimes and tells of his friends who were puzzled all afternoon by the bored professional voice answering his phone: "Hello, Fisher Company at your service. May I help you?"

The chairs are being stacked around us, the lights have been turned up to full, glaring intensity: we are being thrown out. Just before we all enter the limousine, Annie embraces me and whispers in my ear—at last—"My angel, you were superb!"

ARE YOU THE GUY?

The telephone starts ringing early in the morning. It doesn't stop. All of America is calling.

I receive offers to do television commercials, write a children's book, record a song, make a movie, walk across ridiculous sites; magazines battle for an exclusive, impresarios vie to "handle" me. Barely understanding, I keep scribbling notes on little pieces of paper and stacking them. I cry for help to Jim. He's coming tomorrow. We'll sort out the mess. I'll throw out most of the offers. No way will they succeed in changing me into a millionaire!

Jean-Louis and Jean-François head for the airport.
All the way to Paris, they laughingly ask everyone, "How

much?" For Jean-Louis, betrayed by greed, it is the expression that symbolizes the American spirit. Upon landing, he goes directly to the office, as he'd promised his employer.

French newspapers transform my friends into celebrities. When Jean-François returns to his village, what impresses the locals most is that he spent time in a New York City prison. He can't tour the marketplace without being hailed: "Hey, jail-boy!" "How are you doing today, jail-boy?"

"After half a crossing, I knew you were all right. I never saw you so at ease on a cable. You were gliding, magnificent," confides Annie fondly. Finally alone, we plan to have an intimate dinner. But instead of a fine restaurant, it's a hospital we are seeking—Annie's been bitten by one of her cats.

The first person I stop in the street says, "Go east on Twenty-third all the way to First Avenue, make a left, the hospital is right there, but I'm warning you, you won't find any towers over there!" I nod my thanks and keep walking, then pull up short. "Annie, did you understand what that person said? He said *you won't find any towers*. It means he knows who I am. It means he recognized me! Someone recognized me!"

A few minutes later, a lady interrupts our progress. "Excuse me, are you the guy who walked between the twin towers on a tightrope?" I give her an autograph.

Two blocks farther, an old man waiting for the WALK sign stares at me: "Are you the guy who walked?" I'm happy to answer yes.

In front of the hospital, two teenagers bump into us on their way out; instead of a " 'scuse me," I get, "Are you the guy?"

The nurse invites Annie to sit on a stool, looks at her wound, and turns to me, smiling: "Are you . . . ?"

"Oh, yes!" I say with pride. "I am the guy! And if you want to know if it was windy up there, I can assure you it was! What else do you want to know?"

The nurse tilts her head, as if suddenly I have become her mental patient, and completes her query: "Are you . . . related to the injured party?"

Nixon resigns. I barely recognize the name.

Francis sends a telegram: RICHARD IS GONE, PHILIPPE IS KING!

JONNY WHO?

One night at the Village Vanguard, Bob Dylan sings a new song in my honor, "Don't Fall!" I'm sure I've heard of him.

A direct call from Johnny Carson: he wants me on his show. "Johnny who?" I ask, before explaining that I hate television and do not wish to appear on a talk show that gives so little time to its guests and tends to reduce all topics to joke opportunities.

LUNCH OR DINNER

"To endorse Sweet 'N Low? I do not understand what you want. But let me tell you, I'm not sweet and low, I'm harsh and high!" I hang up, hoping Jim will come soon.

The telephone does not stop ringing, the offers keep pouring in, and Jim keeps helping.

By now we're getting professional!

I answer the phone; people are happy and amazed to reach me directly, to hear the sound of my voice. I understand nothing of what they want. So I pass the phone to Jim. (He knows who Nixon, Bob Dylan, and Johnny Carson are.) Jim listens, puts the caller on hold, tells me what it's about, and if I am so inclined, I agree to a meeting. I open my blank date book, flip through the empty pages, and wait. Jim is terribly sorry to announce, "Philippe's next month is completely booked . . . Except at the beginning of next week . . . Yes, we might be able to squeeze in a lunch or a dinner . . . "

Just like that, we're now being fed very well twice a day: to impress me, to win me over, or just because I'm French, the business vultures always take us to great restaurants.

In the beginning, I betray my hatred of commercials, my contempt for product endorsement, even before attacking my entrée. But after a few meals, I learn to pretend that the deal interests me until I've finished my third dessert. Then, after an espresso, I go for the kill: "Let's summarize: to promote your fast-food chain, you want me to walk the wire disguised as a hamburger? Oh, but I will never, ever do that, not even for millions of dollars!"

NUTS AND BOLTS

The engineers painstakingly performed the teardown operation in the rain, starting right after I was taken off the roof. The policemen diligently laid out on the floor every item of equipment, down to the nuts and bolts. They photographed and inventoried it.

I receive duplicates of the paperwork, with an invitation to come pick up what's mine.

Breathing heavily, three bulky policemen bring the miscoiled walk-cable from storage. They are at a loss to understand how two skinny Frenchmen carried it. I'm tempted to take it from them in a quick display of Supermanhood, but I know my body will be severely punished. Since the authorities are playing the restitution game to absurdity—the printed inventory includes (3) USED FLASHBULBS, (1) BOTTLE COVER, (1) TOWEL—I decide to play as well. After carefully scanning the list and checking the equipment, I earnestly declare that there are items missing. After a long moment of confusion, I offer, "Oh, I remember what I'm looking for—the broken helmet, the three gloves, the plastic bags, the cardboard boxes, and most importantly, the large wooden crate—must still be in the towers, hidden!"

I'm given an escort of athletic detectives, all fans quite happy to break the dullness of the day, and up we run. With the excuse of a failing memory, I climb up and down each tower, retracing with delight the forbidden itineraries, even opening a few doors I had not dared to try before. We retrieve the junk and add it to the pile of equipment. I sign the release. My bodyguards load a police van, drive me home, and help bring the ton of equipment into my living room.

The maintenance man raises his eyebrows. I sign autographs.

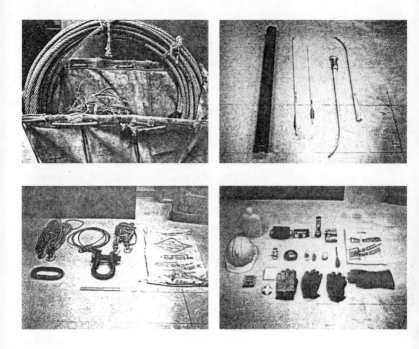

LOTS OF CHALK

The Port Authority of New York and New Jersey makes me an offer I can't refuse. I must explain to the Security Department how I did it. Twelve very serious men in gray suits sit on both sides of a very long table in a very secret conference room. I sit at the end of the table, like a Godfather.

I ask for a blackboard and lots of chalk.

For several hours, I let them have it: I describe the spying, the sneaking, the disguises, the interviews, the deliveries—everything. Almost everything. I sketch itineraries, draw hiding places, scribe arrows pointing at weaknesses in the security system. I answer questions and conclude by offering suggestions on ways to improve security at the World Trade Center.

The audience is grateful and overwhelmed.

I am recognized everywhere. My street-juggling audience has doubled in size. In my mailbox, I find love letters and profound statements from awe-inspired citizens.

Even Albert contacts me.

He is remorseful; he wants to talk, bring part of the money he made selling his pictures for me to pass on to Jean-Louis. Fine. Annie reacts vehemently; she will not allow him in the apartment. When I agree to a meeting on the street, she does not hide her disgust: "Albert wants to see you again because you're a celebrity; you are ready to see him again because you don't like to make enemies."

I feel differently. Notwithstanding the betrayal and the giving up, I know the coup would not have happened without him. So why not let him acknowledge his wrongdoings, and accept his reparations? I go to meet him.

I call Jean-Louis, who says, "Pff! Give the money to Jean-François." Case closed.

CENTRAL PARK

What a great punishment! I twist the sentence of the court—to juggle for small children in a park—into a major high wire walk over Central Park.

Without seeking approval, I announce my intention to the press and invite TV networks to follow my preparations. Unable to curtail my efforts, the politicians happily join the press coverage.

So here I am, under a stormy night sky, ready to set foot on a 600-foot inclined cable anchored to a tree at one end of Belvedere Lake, rising above the water and arriving 80 feet in the air at a tiny window atop the tower of Belvedere Castle.

Five thousand cheerful New Yorkers are waiting.

The sky opens and pours endless thick rain. The politicians do not know what to do. I grab their megaphone and address the crowd: "Friends! You could stay and watch. I could walk under the pouring rain. But the walk would not be beautiful. And it would not be pleasant for you and for me. So come back tomorrow—same place, same time—for a wonderful evening and a great walk!" Thunderous applause competes with thunder. Running in the mud, the crowd disperses. The politicians look at each other and improvise a press conference under umbrellas.

AFTER

Shall I tell the truth? I send Annie back to France. I don't want anything to dull the splendor of my newfound fame, to slow the unrestrained and joyous tempo of my new beginning.

America has saluted me.

New York City adopts me.

I stay.

I discover the city by myself, impatiently.

I incessantly defend against cops and vagrants my new street-juggling territories: Sheridan Square in the Village at night, Washington Square Park by day.

Jim Moore welcomes me as a roommate in his airy, well-lit loft on Hudson Street, a cable-tow's length from my cherished twin towers. There, years later, my friend the painter Elaine Fasula creates a masterpiece: we rejoice in the home birth of our daughter, Cordia-Gypsy.

Looking for more marvels, I stumble upon an unfinished Gothic cathedral uptown and fall in love. Following a surprise walk high above the nave for a few friends, I bring the facade of the Cathedral Church of St. John the Divine to the attention of millions by walking across Amsterdam Avenue from a sixteen-story building to the base of the yet-to-be-built north tower. I come bearing to the bishop and the dean the golden trowel that was used in 1892 to cement the cathedral's first stone. "Following a forty-year hiatus, the cathedral builds again!" announces the caption under a large photograph gracing the front page of *The New York Times* on September 30, 1982.

I become an Artist-In-Residence at the cathedral, which provides an office and shelters my equipment and archives. I continue to offer my art to the church, staging performances inside and outside, raising funds for, and awareness of, its numerous programs. Traveling around the world, I become something of an ambassador of St. John the Divine. And twice a year—it's become a tradition—I play maintenance man and change the 150 bulbs of the chandeliers of Synod Hall, where my practice wire is invisibly set between balconies.

The red PROJECTS box has emigrated from rue Laplace to St. John the Divine. It sleeps with my archives, protected from the agitation of the world by three feet of granite.

One day, I slide my hand into the box and retrieve a forgotten file on canyons. Several journeys to Arizona, numerous meetings with my brothers the Navajo Indians, and the work-in-progress *Canyon Walk* is born. It is an opera performed on a high wire

rigged from one rim of the Little Colorado River Gorge (an over-looked gem of the Navajo Nation) to a solitary monolith standing 1,600 feet tall, 1,200 feet away.

I will walk from civilization to the unknown. But when? Following seasons of study and preparation, I call without shame: Where are you, patron of the arts, visionary angel? Produce this mythic voyage that will inspire the world!

Oh! Did I forget to mention?

Following my performance between the towers, I am invited to sign the beam on the rooftop of the south tower, the place where the wire and I departed.

I sign in indelible ink, so that the inscription may remain indefinitely.

Guy Tozzoli, the thought-provoking, admirable knight of the World Trade Center project, who is responsible for planning, building, and operating WTC, invites me to his office in the clouds; he congratulates me, lets me know that it was his idea that the judge drop the charges in exchange for a performance, and presents me with a VIP pass to the Observation Deck—"Valid forever."

I go there quite often. I present my towers to my friends, my family. I daydream one more time . . .

Alone, I lean on the fence, facing the other tower, and try to let the walks come back to mind. They never do. The feat was impossible: I have to make an effort of imagination to set the images in motion.

I am the only visitor who ever looks up. I interrogate the sky with the hope of seeing the bird . . . but the bird never returns. He is probably uninterested in seeing me with two feet squarely planted on a slab of concrete, albeit a slab floating in reach of the clouds. Yet I'll keep visiting and dreaming forever, atop my indestructible twin towers.

Forever, or so I think.

PERMANENT   THE PORT AUTHORITY OF NY & NJ   DO NOT COLLECT

THE OBSERVATION DECK AT THE WORLD TRADE CENTER
COMPLIMENTARY ADMISSION PASS

ADMIT *Philippe Petit & Guests*   DATE *Open*

OF

REQUESTED BY

Approved By

PA 3285/12-75   NO. 2584

Twenty-seven years later, instead of gathering memories, I relived the World Trade Center adventure. I became once again the eighteen-year-old, the twenty-four-year-old, forgetting to eat, losing sleep, being frightened or elated, laughing at myself.

I shaped the story with thoughts from my month with Marlon Brando during the filming of his workshop "Lying for a Living"— between takes, I was furiously scribbling my first draft in red ink. This terribly talented master of deceit taught me golden rules I had forgotten I knew, which applied as much to the page as to the stage. By practicing the discipline of self-imposed intellectual immobility—akin to the *respect of stillness* Marlon calls for—I was able to apprehend the essence of each chapter before I drafted it. My pen learned to perceive what lurked on the other side of the action it was busy describing until, like him, I could declare, I *can see a smile in the dark*.

Later, I pinned in front of me "Lessons of Darkness," Werner Herzog's "Minnesota Declaration: Truth and Fact in Documentary Cinema." The single-page text exhorted me to express the "ecstatic truth" about WTC, which is "mysterious and elusive, and can be reached only by . . ."

Then I wrote, listening to another "WTC"—Bach's *Well-Tempered Clavier*, the definitive interpretation by Evelyne Crochet at the piano. Her determination and intensity as she starts the second prelude are the determination and intensity of my first steps. Playing the sixteenth prelude, she masters suspension, like me during my first crossing—in perfect balance, yet vulnerable, alone, and courageous.

I listened to the two books—each of twenty-four preludes and twenty-four fugues—as twin towers. Her monumental recording reflects my encounters with the gods during the eight crossings on the wire. The music inspired me to invent a fundamental rhythm, to compose faithful suites of words instead of suites of faithful words.

As the words filled the pages, I resisted the urge to punctuate the manuscript's progress with joyful returns to street-juggling and high wire escapades. Each day, I looked at the barn I have been building with the methods and tools of eighteenth-century timber framers. I was tempted to start assembling the last two windows and doors. But—*the book, the book, the book . . .*

Of course, without permission, wire walking, juggling, and my usual collection of cherished activities flitted around the manuscript, alighted in the margins, and stared at me, the writer, like newborn birds awaiting the return of a parent, and their silent ruckus imprinted the text as much as the ink from my calligraphy pen.

Suddenly, I stopped writing. My towers were under attack, then destroyed, taking an immense number of lives down with them. Then my cathedral was on fire. Doom. Tempest. Chaos. Reflection. After a while, with rebellion in my blood, I wrote, "As an artist, my mission is to create," and went back to writing.

Above it all, sweeping by when I least expected it—Ah, the wind . . . always the wind!—soothing my struggles, celebrating my achievements, or warmly teasing or simply smiling at me, was the ethereal presence of a little Gypsy girl who flew away from Planet Earth at the age of nine and a half, without warning or regret.

Rest in Peace, Cordia-Gypsy, in the columbarium of the Cathedral St. John the Divine. The recent fire did not scatter your ashes to the four winds—you are here encouraging me to keep writing.

With this book, fly with me.

Between paragraphs, I often thought, *The wire is always ready to kill me by surprise, every step of the way*—did you know that, my little Gypsy? Yet I continued to write as I continue to walk, molding my faith in advance of each step.

Whenever I tackled the impossible and the miraculous of the World Trade Center adventure, I remembered the magician René Lavand—did I ever tell you?—he had only one arm. Poet and extraordinary card manipulator, he baffled fellow illusionists by concluding his brilliant demonstrations with, "What I just showed you can also be done with two hands!"

Whenever I chewed on my pen, lost, desperate for words, it was the contradictions of a life too full I was reading on the ceiling. Tell me, am I wrong to mock vertigo from summit to abyss, to reveal the world as I see it? To scribe my destiny boustrophedon, from left to right then right to left, like the ox pulling the plough in successive furrows? Line after line, I weave my life, I write this book. It knots and breaks, it splices and tightens.

The book is finished. Craving the caress of many more well-tensioned bridges-for-one-day, my soles will resume linking people and places. I have not quit setting cables without permission. I am not yet done with narrow-minded engineers, key-collectors unwilling to unlock doors. I sharpen my rigging knife and, defying gravity, go in search of more sublime, soaring surprises . . .

The child of the trees I was, the skyscraper I became, still wants to *conquer* the world—*explore*, I should say—convinced that the world inside you, inside me, inside those around us is equally rich in marvels and mysteries. So if the devil calls, tell him I'm already at work on my next book, *The Art of the Pickpocket*. And if he shows up, I'll shout this old African proverb that always made you giggle: "Devil, if you enter my house, I will crush your toes!"

You know the day I soar to meet you, Gypsy, they may say of me, "He learned to walk in mid-air."

Aerially yours, that's how I wrote this book.

> Philippe Petit
> The Catskills
> March 7, 2002

COM'ERA, DOV'ERA

In Memoriam

On the morning of September 11, 2001, the twin towers
of the World Trade Center were destroyed.
My towers became our towers. I saw them collapse—
hurling, crushing thousands of lives.
Disbelief preceded sorrow for the obliteration of
the buildings, perplexity descended before rage at
the unbearable loss of life.

Eyes closed, I remember and pay my respects
to the victims and to their families.

Forged by fortuitousness, *forever* is a dangerous word.

On the morning of July 14, 1902, the floating city of Venice woke up to a low-pitched, quavering sound.

Overlooking the square of San Marco, the Campanile, the 325-foot tower that was a symbol of the city's power and prosperity, forever its pride, shivered, shook, and collapsed.

On itself.

Like that.

In a cloud of masonry dust.

A miracle for the busy crossroad—markets unfolding, churches congregating—that no one was hurt.

A kid picked up a brick to look at it. It was unbroken, as were the million others—a miracle of a different sort. The brick was passed to someone else. A human chain soon formed. Each brick was retrieved, cleaned, and stacked.

By evening, it was decided the Campanile would be rebuilt *com'era, dov'era*: as it was, where it was.

Before midnight, posters announcing the news, and printed free of charge by an old typesetter, were pasted all over the city by its proud inhabitants.

A new tower, an exact replica, was inaugurated in 1912.

Remember the World Trade Center tragedy.

Establish a memorial site.

Build again.

Let us pass from hand to hand the bricks of renaissance. Let us print WE SHALL NOT BE DOOMED and paste the message high in the sky, for all in the world to read aloud.

Let us rebuild the twin towers.

We need the fuel of time and money, the mortar of ideas, and the million bricks of everyone's concern. Bring yours.

Here is mine:

I envision the twin towers *com'era, dov'era,* but with a twist, a dash of inventive panache. Architects, please make them more magnificent—try a twist, a quarter turn along their longitudinal axes. Make them higher—yes, one more floor, so they reach 111 stories high. And make them stronger, as well as stronger-looking—smoothing the base outward, like those coffee cups that are impossible to topple, is one way. I'll wait. We'll wait.

When the towers again twin-tickle the clouds, I offer to walk again, to be the expression of the builders' collective voice. Together, we will rejoice in an aerial song of victory. I will carry my life across the wire, as your life, as all our lives, past, present, and future—the lives lost, the lives welcomed since.

We can overcome.

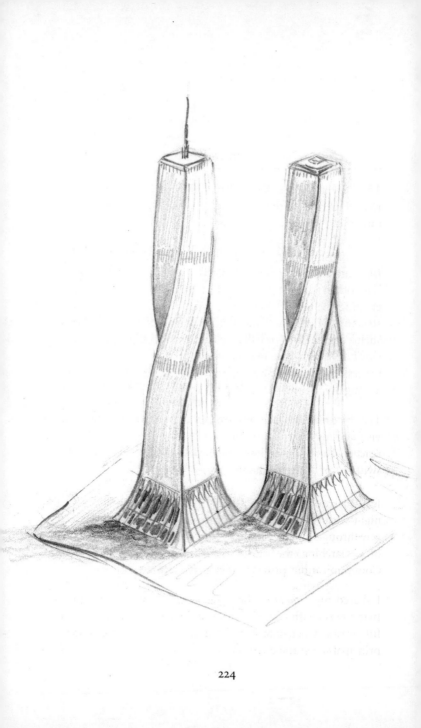

Acknowledgments

The Very Reverend James Parks Morton, my spiritual father, Dean Emeritus of the Cathedral Church of St. John the Divine, once said, "Philippe does not believe in God, but God believes in Philippe." How else would I have been blessed with the superb craftsmanship of the world's best editor, Rebecca Saletan? Our frequent eight-hour-long sessions were joyous brainstormings rather than the bloody combat I had anticipated. Without impoverishing the story or curtailing my style, Becky improved the structure of the book and refined the texture of my writing to such a degree that I owe her a compliment inspired by the film *As Good As It Gets*: "You make me want to be a better writer." In the process, the unbelievable happened: I now count a literary editor among my friends!

Thanks to the continuous support of Andrew Wylie and the vision of my literary agent, Jeffrey Posternak, *To Reach the Clouds* reached North Point Press/Farrar, Straus and Giroux with the swiftness of an arrow shot by Jean-Louis.

Jean-Pierre Pappis of Polaris Images aided me literally day and night with the illustrations. When it came to maneuvering my way through my vast archive of film and video—an essential part of researching the story—John Love and his New Vision Communications provided invaluable technical help.

I shared my concerns about technical accuracy regarding the twin towers with Guy F. Tozzoli, and received, along with colorful stories, a personal introduction to Leslie E. Robertson, the principal structural engineer.

During the writing of this book (and before), Jay Goerk, Judith Friedlaender, Debra Winger, and Joe DeBellis contributed a resource I know little about—money—exemplifying friendship at its most generous.

What do you call an invitation to break bread with the best restaurateurs in the world—culinary friendship? Thank you Karen and David Waltuck, along with Sara and Jake, for opening your home to Kathy and me, and for the earthly delights from your sublime Chanterelle.

Valerie Fanarjian, inspiring Catskills artist of vast talent, opened her heart and her home to encourage the author—the public reading she organized helped me put the manuscript to the test.

Elaine Fasula, Steve Moore, and little Raimi the frog-hunter in their house at the top of the hill were always eager to share their *pasta al pesto* on short notice, and to listen to the latest chapters-in-progress.

A storm fells a tree, cutting power? My neighbor T.J. Kellogg, with his wife, Charlene, their children, and his backhoe, was a speedy warrior against the forces of nature that tried to prevent me from writing.

A few miles away, renaissance artist John Kahn offered myriad forms of friendship and support. On the other side of the ocean, Dr. Catherine Dolto, my *Valet d'Epée*, knows my every move, and waits with love to assist me.

Living legend Francis Brunn, performer extraordinaire Nathalie Enterline, and flamenco guitarist Raphael Brunn were the perfect Manhattan hosts during the period of numerous meetings with my publisher. Francis and I have brought the art of interruption to new heights, but his opinions, even expressed in the heat of our crisscrossing monologues, carried weight with me and influenced the book.

A special bow of gratitude to producer-director James Signorelli, who was the first to believe in this "true crime" story, and who helped so much in assembling the mosaic of information I needed to write it.

Welcome to the Right Reverend Mark S. Sisk, fifteenth Bishop of New York, and to the Very Reverend Dr. James A. Kowalski, ninth Dean of the Cathedral Church of St. John the Divine. I cannot wait to start daydreaming about new projects in my triforium office at the Cathedral, which I salute and thank here for continuing to shelter and inspire this poet-of-the sky.

To Reach the Clouds opens and closes with an immense thank you to Kathy O'Donnell. Only she and I know how many words were processed, copied, challenged, replaced, retyped and changed again, all with her unflagging literary expertise and energy. I am eager to work with her on the next book, on the next walk.